Helpful Guide To Understanding "The Chosen" Season Two

Dr. Rick Gillespie-Mobley

Copyright © 2023 Rick Gillespie-Mobley

All rights reserved.

DEDICATION

I dedicate this book to all the people I have been blessed to serve as their pastor at Roxbury Presbyterian Church, Glenville Presbyterian Church, Glenville New Life Community Church, New Life Fellowship, Calvary Presbyterian Church, and New Life At Calvary.

CONTENTS

	Introduction	vi
	Actual Biblical Characters Appearing In Seasons 1 & 2	viii
1	Resources For Episode 1 Thunder	Pg 1
2	Resources For Episode 2 I Saw You	Pg 13
3	Resources For Episode 3 Matthew 4:24	Pg 25
4	Resources For Episode 4 Perfect Opportunity	Pg 33
5	Resources For Episode 5 Spirit	Pg 45
6	Resources For Episode 6 Unlawful	Pg 58
7	Resources For Episode 7 Reckoning	Pg 69
8	Resources For Episode 8 Beyond Mountains	Pg 77
9	Resources For Episode Christmas Messengers	Pg 86
10	About The Author	Pg 94

ACKNOWLEDGMENTS

I want to acknowledge that without Jesus Christ as Lord of my life, this book and so many other things I have done, would not have been possible. To God By The Glory.

Introduction Season 2

One of the purposes of "The Chosen" is to create characters with depth of life so that you can read the scriptures and understand why biblical characters may behave in the way that they do. "The Chosen" is not a biblical story as revealed in the Scriptures, but it is a story which contains the Scriptures and provides us with a possibility of how things may have taken place. If you accept it for what it is, you will be strengthened and encouraged in your faith. If you demand it be a literal rendition of the Scriptures, you will be disappointed in your search. "The Chosen" is a wonderful way to capture the heart, the emotions, and the essence of the characters in the Scriptures.

The purpose of this book is to help you understand how the Scriptures are woven into the story and to learn from both the lives of the characters and the teachings of Scripture. By providing you with a summary of the main characters in each episode, a summary of the content of the episode, and the Scriptures referred to in in the episode, you will be able to glean a greater understanding of what is happening as you watch.

There are questions for discussion that you can use in a small group if you choose to use "The Chosen" as a bible study topic. The questions do not require a scholarly background to lead the discussion. The questions are a combination of your reactions to the characters and your application of the Scriptures. The number of questions you will use will depend on the size of your group and whether or not you have watched the episodes prior to meeting or not. Obviously, you will have more time for discussion if you watch the episodes prior to coming together.

"The Chosen" episodes are available for purchase on Amazon.com on dvd. The episodes can be watched for free on the on the Chosen website https://watch.thechosen.tv/. The episodes are also available for free on the Angel Studios App for phones and on the Angel Studio website at https://www.angel.com/watch/the-chosen.

Helpful Guide To Understanding "The Chosen" Season 2

Actual Biblical Characters Appearing In The Chosen Seasons 1 & 2

Ahimelek

14 Ahimelek answered the king, "Who of all your servants is as loyal as David, the king's son-in-law, captain of your bodyguard and highly respected in your household? 15 Was that day the first time I inquired of God for him? Of course not! Let not the king accuse your servant or any of his father's family, for your servant knows nothing at all about this whole affair." <u>The New International Version</u> (Grand Rapids, MI: Zondervan, 2011), 1 Sa 22:14–15.

Andrew

40 Andrew, Simon Peter's brother, was one of the two who heard what John had said and who had followed Jesus. 41 The first thing Andrew did was to find his brother Simon and tell him, "We have found the Messiah" (that is, the Christ). 42 And he brought him to Jesus. <u>The New International Version</u> (Grand Rapids, MI: Zondervan, 2011), Jn 1:40–42.

David

David went to Nob, to Ahimelek the priest. Ahimelek trembled when he met him, and asked, "Why are you alone? Why is no one with you?" 2 David answered Ahimelek the priest, "The king sent me on a mission and said to me, 'No one is to know anything about the mission I am sending you on.' As for my men, I have told them to meet me at a certain place. 3 Now then, what do you have on hand? Give me five loaves of bread, or whatever you can find." <u>The New International Version</u> (Grand Rapids, MI: Zondervan, 2011), 1 Sa 21:1–3.

Jacob

5 So he came to a town in Samaria called Sychar, near the plot of ground Jacob had given to his son Joseph. 6 Jacob's well was there, and Jesus, tired as he was from the journey, sat down by the well. It was about noon. *The New International Version* (Grand Rapids, MI: Zondervan, 2011), Jn 4:5–6.

James son of Alphaeus (Little James)

2 These are the names of the twelve apostles: first, Simon (who is called Peter) and his brother Andrew; James son of Zebedee, and his brother John; 3 Philip and Bartholomew; Thomas and Matthew the tax collector; James son of Alphaeus, and Thaddaeus; 4 Simon the Zealot and Judas Iscariot, who betrayed him.

James son of Zebedee (Big James)

21 Going on from there, he saw two other brothers, James son of Zebedee and his brother John. They were in a boat with their father Zebedee, preparing their nets. Jesus called them, 22 and immediately they left the boat and their father and followed him. *The New International Version* (Grand Rapids, MI: Zondervan, 2011), Mt 4:21–22.

Jesus As Twelve Year Old

41 Every year Jesus' parents went to Jerusalem for the Festival of the Passover. 42 When he was twelve years old, they went up to the festival, according to the custom. 43 After the festival was over, while his parents were returning home, the boy Jesus stayed behind in Jerusalem, but they were unaware of it

Jesus

35 The next day John was there again with two of his disciples. 36 When he saw Jesus passing by, he said, "Look, the Lamb of God!" 37 When the two disciples heard him say this, they followed Jesus. *The New International Version* (Grand Rapids, MI:

Zondervan, 2011), Jn 1:35–37.

John
21 Going on from there, he saw two other brothers, James son of Zebedee and his brother John. They were in a boat with their father Zebedee, preparing their nets. Jesus called them, 22 and immediately they left the boat and their father and followed him. *The New International Version* (Grand Rapids, MI: Zondervan, 2011), Mt 4:21–22.

John The Baptist
In those days John the Baptist came, preaching in the wilderness of Judea 2 and saying, "Repent, for the kingdom of heaven has come near." 3 This is he who was spoken of through the prophet Isaiah: "A voice of one calling in the wilderness, 'Prepare the way for the Lord, make straight paths for him.'" *The New International Version* (Grand Rapids, MI: Zondervan, 2011), Mt 3:1–3.

Joseph
48 When his parents saw him, they were astonished. His mother said to him, "Son, why have you treated us like this? Your father and I have been anxiously searching for you." *The New International Version* (Grand Rapids, MI: Zondervan, 2011), Lk 2:48.

Joshua

13 Then Moses set out with Joshua his aide, and Moses went up on the mountain of God *The New International Version* (Grand Rapids, MI: Zondervan, 2011), Ex 24:13.

Lazarus

9 Meanwhile a large crowd of Jews found out that Jesus was there and came, not only because of him but also to see Lazarus, whom he had raised from the dead. 10 So the chief priests made plans to kill Lazarus as well, 11 for on account of him many of the Jews were

going over to Jesus and believing in him.

Luke

Many have undertaken to draw up an account of the things that have been fulfilled among us, 2 just as they were handed down to us by those who from the first were eyewitnesses and servants of the word. 3 With this in mind, since I myself have carefully investigated everything from the beginning, I too decided to write an orderly account for you, most excellent Theophilus, 4 so that you may know the certainty of the things you have been taught. *The New International Version* (Grand Rapids, MI: Zondervan, 2011), Lk 1:1–4.

Man Healed At The Pool Of Bethesda (Jesse)

5 Some time later, Jesus went up to Jerusalem for one of the Jewish festivals. 2 Now there is in Jerusalem near the Sheep Gate a pool, which in Aramaic is called Bethesda and which is surrounded by five covered colonnades. 3 Here a great number of disabled people used to lie—the blind, the lame, the paralyzed. [4] 5 One who was there had been an invalid for thirty-eight years. 6 When Jesus saw him lying there and learned that he had been in this condition for a long time, he asked him, "Do you want to get well?" *The New International Version* (Grand Rapids, MI: Zondervan, 2011), Jn 5:1–6.

Mary

48 When his parents saw him, they were astonished. His mother said to him, "Son, why have you treated us like this? Your father and I have been anxiously searching for you." *The New International Version* (Grand Rapids, MI: Zondervan, 2011), Lk 2:48.

Mary Magdalene

After this, Jesus traveled about from one town and village to another, proclaiming the good news of the kingdom of God. The Twelve were with him, 2 and also some women who had been cured of evil spirits and diseases: Mary (called Magdalene) from whom seven demons had come out; 3 Joanna the wife of Chuza, the manager of Herod's household; Susanna; and many others. These women were helping to support them out of their own means. _The New International Version_ (Grand Rapids, MI: Zondervan, 2011), Lk 8:1–3.

Matthew

10 While Jesus was having dinner at Matthew's house, many tax collectors and sinners came and ate with him and his disciples. 11 When the Pharisees saw this, they asked his disciples, "Why does your teacher eat with tax collectors and sinners?" _The New International Version_ (Grand Rapids, MI: Zondervan, 2011), Mt 9:10–11.

Moses

" So Moses prayed for the people. 8 The Lord said to Moses, "Make a snake and put it up on a pole; anyone who is bitten can look at it and live." 9 So Moses made a bronze snake and put it up on a pole. Then when anyone was bitten by a snake and looked at the bronze snake, they lived.

Nathanael

47 When Jesus saw Nathanael approaching, he said of him, "Here truly is an Israelite in whom there is no deceit." 48 "How do you know me?" Nathanael asked. Jesus answered, "I saw you while you were still under the fig tree before Philip called you." 49 Then Nathanael declared, "Rabbi, you are the Son of God; you are the king of Israel." 50 Jesus said, "You _The New International Version_ (Grand Rapids, MI: Zondervan, 2011), Jn 1:47–50.

Nicodemus

"Now there was a Pharisee, a man named Nicodemus who was a member of the Jewish ruling council. 2 He came to Jesus at night and said, "Rabbi, we know that you are a teacher who has come from God. For no one could perform the signs you are doing if God were not with him."" *The New International Version* (Grand Rapids, MI: Zondervan, 2011), Jn 3:1–2.

38 Later, Joseph of Arimathea asked Pilate for the body of Jesus. Now Joseph was a disciple of Jesus, but secretly because he feared the Jewish leaders. With Pilate's permission, he came and took the body away. 39 He was accompanied by Nicodemus, the man who earlier had visited Jesus at night. Nicodemus brought a mixture of myrrh and aloes, about seventy-five pounds. 40 Taking Jesus' body, the two of them wrapped it, with the spices, in strips of linen. This was in accordance with Jewish burial customs *The New International Version* (Grand Rapids, MI: Zondervan, 2011), Jn 19:38–40.

Phillip

43 The next day Jesus decided to leave for Galilee. Finding Philip, he said to him, "Follow me." 44 Philip, like Andrew and Peter, was from the town of Bethsaida. 45 Philip found Nathanael and told him, "We have found the one Moses wrote about in the Law, and about whom the prophets also wrote—Jesus of Nazareth, the son of Joseph."*The New International Version* (Grand Rapids, MI: Zondervan, 2011), Jn 1:43–45.

Simon

40 Andrew, Simon Peter's brother, was one of the two who heard what John had said and who had followed Jesus. 41 The first thing

Andrew did was to find his brother Simon and tell him, "We have found the Messiah" (that is, the Christ). 42 And he brought him to Jesus. *The New International Version* (Grand Rapids, MI: Zondervan, 2011), Jn 1:40–42.

Simon The Zealot

those he wanted, and they came to him. 14 He appointed twelve that they might be with him and that he might send them out to preach 15 and to have authority to drive out demons. 16 These are the twelve he appointed: Simon (to whom he gave the name Peter), 17 James son of Zebedee and his brother John (to them he gave the name Boanerges, which means "sons of thunder"), 18 Andrew, Philip, Bartholomew, Matthew, Thomas, James son of Alphaeus, Thaddaeus, Simon the Zealot 19 and Judas Iscariot, who betrayed him *The New International Version* (Grand Rapids, MI: Zondervan, 2011), Mk 3:13–19.

Simon's Wife (Eden)

14 When Jesus came into Peter's house, he saw Peter's mother-in-law lying in bed with a fever. 15 He touched her hand and the fever left her, and she got up and began to wait on him. *The New International Version* (Grand Rapids, MI: Zondervan, 2011), Mt 8:14–15.

5 Don't we have the right to take a believing wife along with us, as do the other apostles and the Lord's brothers and Cephas?*The New International Version* (Grand Rapids, MI: Zondervan, 2011), 1 Co 9:5.

Thaddaeus

2 These are the names of the twelve apostles: first, Simon (who is called Peter) and his brother Andrew; James son of Zebedee, and his

brother John; 3 Philip and Bartholomew; Thomas and Matthew the tax collector; James son of Alphaeus, and Thaddaeus; 4 Simon the Zealot and Judas Iscariot, who betrayed him.

The Man With Leprosy
2 A man with leprosy came and knelt before him and said, "Lord, if you are willing, you can make me clean." *The New International Version* (Grand Rapids, MI: Zondervan, 2011), Mt 8:1–2.

The Man With The Shriveled Hand (Elam)
Then Jesus said to them, "The Son of Man is Lord of the Sabbath." 6 On another Sabbath he went into the synagogue and was teaching, and a man was there whose right hand was shriveled. 7 The Pharisees and the teachers of the law were looking for a reason to accuse Jesus, so they watched him closely to see if he would heal on the Sabbath. 8 But Jesus knew what they were thinking and said to the man with the shriveled hand, "Get up and stand in front of everyone." So he got up and stood there. 9 Then Jesus said to them, "I ask you, which is lawful on the Sabbath: to do good or to do evil, to save life or to destroy it?" 10 He looked around at them all, and then said to the man, "Stretch out your hand." He did so, and his hand was completely restored. 11 But the Pharisees and the teachers of the *The New International Version* (Grand Rapids, MI: Zondervan, 2011), Lk 6:5–11.

The Men Bringing In The Paralyzed Man and The Paralyzed Man
Some men came, bringing to him a paralyzed man, carried by four of them. 4 Since they could not get him to Jesus because of the crowd, they made an opening in the roof above Jesus by digging through it and then lowered the mat the man was lying on. *The New International Version* (Grand Rapids, MI: Zondervan, 2011), Mk 2:3–4.

The Woman At The Well
28 Then, leaving her water jar, the woman went back to the town and said to the people, 29 "Come, see a man who told me everything I ever did. Could this be the Messiah?" 30 They came out of the town and made their way toward him. *The New International Version* (Grand Rapids, MI: Zondervan, 2011), Jn 4:28–30.

Thomas
24 Now Thomas (also known as Didymus), one of the Twelve, was not with the disciples when Jesus came. 25 So the other disciples told him, "We have seen the Lord!" But he said to them, "Unless I see the nail marks in his hands and put my finger where the nails were, and put my hand into his side, I will not believe." *The New International Version* (Grand Rapids, MI: Zondervan, 2011), Jn 20:24–25.

Zebedee

19 When he had gone a little farther, he saw James son of Zebedee and his brother John in a boat, preparing their nets. 20 Without delay he called them, and they left their father Zebedee in the boat with the hired men and followed him.

RESOURCES FOR EPISODE 1 THUNDER

Season 2 Episode 1 Thunder
1 Hour 4 Minutes Viewing Time

The Main Characters

James (Big James) the brother of John has changed actors from Season 1
Disciples 30 Years Later—the disciples share their story of how they met Jesus.

Mary—Jesus' mother who encourages John to write the story of Jesus.

James & John—the disciples assigned to plow a field by Jesus.

Thomas—the one who leaves his wine business and joins Jesus and the disciples to become one of the twelve.

Rhema—the former business partner of Thomas from the wedding in Cana story and she also comes to follow Jesus.

Kofney—Rhema's father who is grateful to Jesus for saving his business reputation, but absolutely opposed to Rhema and Thomas following Jesus.

The Disciples—the followers of Jesus who struggle to get Jesus to follow a schedule, they argue over who is in charge, and they think they are responsible for Jesus.

Jesus—the one who teaches the Samaritans, tries to move the

disciples beyond their prejudice, heals, and demonstrates God's unbelievable mercy for all.

Big James & John—the brothers who plow and plant a field, and who are given the name Sons of Thunder due to their prejudice and anger.

Melek--the Samaritan with a broken leg who feels very unworthy of God's love.

Furkina—the name given to the woman at the well who can't stop telling others about Jesus. She invites Jesus and the disciples to her home for their final night in Samaria.

Samaritans—several different groups who seek to throw stones at or verbally attack the Jews on several occasions.

Gershon—the Samaritan priest of Sychar who invites Jesus to read from the Torah at the synagogue before he leaves Samaria.

Summary Of Season 2 Episode 1 Thunder

The episode opens in the future after the resurrection has taken place and the disciples have gotten much older. John is collecting the stories from each of the disciples, Mary Magdalene, and Mary, Jesus's mom on how they first met Jesus. It is obvious that he is going to write a book about them and the things that Jesus did while he was with them. There are hints that everybody was expecting Matthew to write a book since he was always taking notes. John struggles with how he should begin the book he is going to write because he does not know how far back in time he should go.

The scene goes back to the time line of the previous episode in which Jesus and the disciples are in Samaria after the encounter of the woman at the well. John and Big James have been instructed by Jesus to plow and field. They are happy for the assignment, because they don't want to be near any Samaritans. They consider themselves blessed and special to have received the assignment from Jesus.

The other disciples have been sent into town by Jesus. They are excited because crowds are gathering to hear more of Jesus' preaching. They go to inform Jesus of the crowd only to discover that Jesus is no longer in the house. They organize search parties among themselves in order to find Jesus. Matthew is asked to remain at the house in case Jesus arrives.

Thomas, Rhema, and her father Kofney come to Sychar to find Jesus. They are insulted by Samaritans. When they arrive at the house where Matthew is, they get less than a warm welcome from Matthew. Mary arrives just as Thomas is ready to slam the door in their faces, and she welcomes them in properly. It is obvious that Kofney is opposed to coming to Sychar.

Matthew and Thomas are both former businessmen given to details, numbers and schedules. When Thomas says maybe Jesus called him so that he could use his skills to organize things, Matthew looks a little worried. Big James and John arrive at the house having completed their work in the fields.

Jesus has been helping a man who is so impressed with Jesus' carpentry skills that he asks Jesus to consider opening a shop in town. Jesus is later seen teaching the people using the parable of the lost sheep from among the 100. Jesus speaks of the joy of having one sinner repent.

The scene shifts to a man with a crutch who is surprised to see his field plowed and planted. He has no idea what has taken place. The scene then shifts back to Jesus and the disciples entering the home after the preaching has taken place. Jesus welcomes Thomas and Rhema. Rhema introduces Jesus to her father, Kofney. Kofney demands to have a meeting with Jesus.

Jesus informs the others that Big James and John have done a wonderful act of service and they are to tell the others what they have done. Trouble starts to brew the next day among the disciples, because Big James and John seem to have taken a position of leadership among the group. Jesus has given them assignments to give to the others on purchasing some items. There are feelings of jealousy arising among the disciples.

Simon runs into Furkina (woman at the well), and she asks him to give an invitation to Jesus for her. Meanwhile, Jesus and Kofney have a one on one meeting. Jesus is patient with Kofney, who is very hostile toward him. He appreciates that Jesus saved his business reputation by helping out at the wedding in Cana, but he will not give Jesus his belief or devotion. Jesus has tears in his eyes when Kofney leaves him.

Kofney assures Thomas that he is being foolish. He predicts Thomas would one day ask for his daughter Rhema hand in marriage, but he can't guarantee what he will say at that point. Rhema is greatly saddened at her father's departure.

Big James and John find Jesus near the field they plowed and he congratulates them on a job well done. He tells them that Melek, the man who owned the house owes them a great debt of gratitude. James and John are surprised to learn whose field they had planted.

Jesus invites himself and the disciples to Melek's house for dinner and he brings the food to feed everyone. Melek's wife wants to know, if Jesus is the Messiah, when will the pain and suffering end. Jesus explains his kingdom. Melek share's his story of how his leg was broken. He feels so unworthy and beyond the love of God. He carries a huge burden of guilt. Jesus surprises him with his response.

After dinner they return to the city and accepts Furkina's invitation. She and her husband welcome them in. In the morning, Melek and his family have a joyful celebration together. The disciples learn even more of the power of Jesus. Yet, the disciples insist on trying to get Jesus to follow a logical plan of action for the ministry.

Big James and John find Jesus on the road. They are attacked by a group of Samaritans. James and John want to call fire down from heaven. Jesus gives them the names the Sons of Thunder. Jesus has a lesson for them in sowing seeds for the future.

Gershon, the priest of Sychar, invites Jesus to do the reading from the Torah. Jesus asks John to come assist him in choosing the passage. The passage Jesus chooses ties into the passage that John chooses for his opening in the gospel of John. This ties the beginning of the episode to the end of the episode.

Scriptures Woven Into Season 2 Episode 1 Thunder

34 Truly I tell you, this generation will certainly not pass away until all these things have happened. 35 Heaven and earth will pass away, but my words will never pass away. *The New International Version* (Grand Rapids, MI: Zondervan, 2011), Mt 24:34–36.

30 Jesus performed many other signs in the presence of his disciples, which are not recorded in this book. 31 But these are written that you may believe that Jesus is the Messiah, the Son of God, and that by believing you may have life in his name. *The New International Version* (Grand Rapids, MI: Zondervan, 2011), Jn 20:30–31.

39 Many of the Samaritans from that town believed in him because of the woman's testimony, "He told me everything I ever did." 40 So when the Samaritans came to him, they urged him to stay with them, and he stayed two days. 41 And because of his words many more became believers. 42 They said to the woman, "We no longer believe just because of what you said; now we have heard for ourselves, and we know that this man really is the Savior of the world."
The New International Version (Grand Rapids, MI: Zondervan, 2011), Jn 4:39–42.

On the third day a wedding took place at Cana in Galilee. Jesus' mother was there, 2 and Jesus and his disciples had also been invited to the wedding. 3 When the wine was gone, Jesus' mother said to him, "They have no more wine." 4 "Woman, why do you involve me?" Jesus replied. "My hour has not yet come." 5 His mother said to the servants, "Do whatever he tells you." 6 Nearby stood six stone water jars, the kind used by the Jews for ceremonial washing, each holding from twenty to thirty gallons. 7 Jesus said to the servants, "Fill the jars with water"; so they filled them to the brim. 8 Then he told them, "Now draw some out and take it to the master of the banquet." They did so, 9 and the master of the banquet tasted the water that had been turned into wine. He did not realize where it had come from, though the servants who had drawn the water knew. Then he called the bridegroom aside 10 and said, "Everyone brings out the choice wine first and then the cheaper wine after the guests have had too much to drink; but you have saved the best till now." 11 What Jesus did here in Cana of Galilee was the first of the signs through which he revealed his glory; and his disciples believed in him. *The New International Version* (Grand Rapids, MI: Zondervan, 2011), Jn 2:1–11.

17 On hearing this, Jesus said to them, "It is not the healthy who need a doctor, but the sick. I have not come to call the righteous, but sinners." *The New International Version* (Grand Rapids, MI: Zondervan, 2011), Mk 2:17.

3 Then Jesus told them this parable: 4 "Suppose one of you has a hundred sheep and loses one of them. Doesn't he leave the ninety-nine in the open country and go after the lost sheep until he finds it? 5 And when he finds it, he joyfully puts it on his shoulders 6 and goes home. Then he calls his friends and neighbors together and says, 'Rejoice with me; I have found my lost sheep.' 7 I tell you that in the same way there will be more rejoicing in heaven over one sinner who repents than over ninety-nine righteous persons who do not need to repent. *The New International Version* (Grand Rapids, MI: Zondervan, 2011), Luke 15:3-7

37 "Anyone who loves their father or mother more than me is not worthy of me; anyone who loves their son or daughter more than me is not worthy of me. 38 Whoever does not take up their cross and follow me is not worthy of me. 39 Whoever finds their life will lose it, and whoever loses their life for my sake will find it. *The New International Version* (Grand Rapids, MI: Zondervan, 2011), Mt 10:37–39.

36 Jesus said, "My kingdom is not of this world. If it were, my servants would fight to prevent my arrest by the Jewish leaders. But now my kingdom is from another place.*The New International Version* (Grand Rapids, MI: Zondervan, 2011), Jn 18:36.

30 In reply Jesus said: "A man was going down from Jerusalem to Jericho, when he was attacked by robbers. They stripped him of his clothes, beat him and went away, leaving him half dead. 31 A priest happened to be going down the same road, and when he saw the man, he passed by on the other side. 32 So too, a Levite, when he came to the place and saw him, passed by on the other side. 33 But a Samaritan, as he traveled, came where the man was; and when he saw him, he took pity on him. 34 He went to him and bandaged his wounds, pouring on oil and wine. Then he put the man on his own donkey, brought him to an inn and took care of him. 35 The next

day he took out two denarii and gave them to the innkeeper. 'Look after him,' he said, 'and when I return, I will reimburse you for any extra expense you may have.' 36 "Which of these three do you think was a neighbor to the man who fell into the hands of robbers?" 37 The expert in the law replied, "The one who had mercy on him." Jesus told him, "Go and do likewise." *The New International Version* (Grand Rapids, MI: Zondervan, 2011), Lk 10:30–38.

52 And he sent messengers on ahead, who went into a Samaritan village to get things ready for him; 53 but the people there did not welcome him, because he was heading for Jerusalem. 54 When the disciples James and John saw this, they asked, "Lord, do you want us to call fire down from heaven to destroy them?" 55 But Jesus turned and rebuked them. *The New International Version* (Grand Rapids, MI: Zondervan, 2011), Lk 9:52-55.

16 These are the twelve he appointed: Simon (to whom he gave the name Peter), 17 James son of Zebedee and his brother John (to them he gave the name Boanerges, which means "sons of thunder"), 18 Andrew, Philip, Bartholomew, Matthew, Thomas, James son of Alphaeus, Thaddaeus, Simon the Zealot 19 and Judas Iscariot, who betrayed him. *The New International Version* (Grand Rapids, MI: Zondervan, 2011), Mk 3:16–19.

In the beginning God created the heavens and the earth. 2 Now the earth was formless and empty, darkness was over the surface of the deep, and the Spirit of God was hovering over the waters. 3 And God said, "Let there be light," and there was light. 4 God saw that the light was good, and he separated the light from the darkness. 5 God called the light "day," and the darkness he called "night." And there was evening, and there was morning—the first day. *The New International Version* (Grand Rapids, MI: Zondervan, 2011), Ge 1:1–5.

In the beginning was the Word, and the Word was with God, and the Word was God. 2 He was with God in the beginning. 3 Through him all things were made; without him nothing was made that has been made. 4 In him was life, and that life was the light of all mankind. 5 The light shines in the darkness, and the darkness has not overcome it. *The New International Version* (Grand Rapids, MI: Zondervan, 2011), Jn 1:1–5.

Biblical Characters Who Are A Part of Season 2 Episode 1
Thunder

The Older Disciples
The disciples do age, but the bible only provides us with glimpses of Simon and John in the distant future. The scene of John interviewing the disciples in preparation for the writing of the gospel of John is not found in the Scriptures.

Mary
Jesus' mother is an actual biblical character, but the Scriptures do not include an account of her helping John with the opening of the gospel of John.

James and John
James and John are real characters, and they are recorded in Scriptures as wanting Jesus to call down fire from heaven upon the Samaritans. Jesus does give them the nickname "Sons of Thunder", however it is not clear if it is because of this one incident or some other reason. The Scriptures do not record them as clearing a field or taking a leadership role with the disciples in the beginning.

Thomas
Thomas is an actual biblical character who becomes one of the followers of Jesus, best known for his unwillingness to believe in the resurrection until he puts his hand in his side and his fingers in the holes in his hands. The Scriptures do not record the circumstances under which Thomas becomes a disciple, and there is nothing to suggest his occupation before coming to Jesus.

Matthew, Simon, Big James, John, Andrew, Thaddeus, James, Thomas, Mary Magdalene
The disciples are all biblical characters, but the Scriptures do not indicate what they did during the two days they were in Samaria.

Jesus

Jesus is an actual biblical character. His teaching on the Lost Sheep is found in the Scriptures. His ability to heal without being present is recorded in the Scriptures. His staying in Samaria for two extra days is also in the Scriptures along with knowledge of the man robbed, beaten and not dying can be aligned with the parable of the good Samaritan. Jesus does name James and John the "Sons of Thunder," though it appears to happen at a later point in his ministry. Surely the woman at the well has a name, but the Scriptures do not record it. Jesus is the first to call her Furkina. The Scriptures do not tell us what Jesus did during the two days in Samaria so the characters Rhema, Kofney, Gershon, Melek and his family, and Furkina's husband are not recorded in the Scriptures.

Bible Study Discussion Questions Season 2 Episode 1 Thunder

1. When the episode begins in the opening, what's the purpose of the fish swimming in one direction and then fish turning blue and heading in the opposite direction?

2. James and John emphasized their dislike for the Samaritans throughout this episode. Why do we still have prejudice in us even after coming to Jesus?

3. Is it possible to develop new prejudices against people even after coming to know Christ? Why or why not?

4. Why is Rhema's father, Kofney, so angry and upset each time he appears in the episode?

5. What can we learn from Jesus' reaction to Kofney on dealing with angry hurting people?

6. Jesus calls the woman at the well by the name Furkina. What traits do you find admirable in her?

7. Jesus makes the statement, "I demand much from my followers, but very little from others." Why do we demand much from those who have not chosen to follow Jesus?

8. What do you think of Matthew's initial reception of Thomas, Rhema and Kofney?

9. Jesus mentions leaving the 99 in order to go after the one who has wandered away. What makes it difficult for us to go after the person who has walked away from the church?

10. What price does Rhema have to pay in order to follow Jesus? Whom did you have to leave behind in order to follow Jesus?

11. Kofney tells Jesus, that he is thankful for his help, but he cannot give him his belief or devotion. How are people still like Kofney today?

12. Why do you think Big James and John worked so hard in the field assigned to them by Jesus? What do you think went through their minds when they discovered they had been working for a Samaritan?

13. Why is it important to give our best when given an assignment by Jesus?

14. Why does Melek think Jesus does not know what his background truly is?

15. Why is God's grace bigger than our past, and what hope does that give to you?

16. Do you think your first reaction would have been similar to James' and John's if you had been pelted with rocks and spit upon by the Samaritans?

17. Why can we not allow the divisions of our society to keep us from disliking a group of people?

18. Who were some people who had some unexpected changes of hearts in this episode?

19. What was your most favorite thing done by Jesus in this episode?

20. Who could you identify with most in this episode?

2 RESOURCES FOR EPISODE 2 I SAW YOU

Season 2 Episode 2 I Saw You

53 Minutes Duration

Main Characters

Nathanael—young Jewish man who beats the odds to become an architect and receives a Roman commission to design a building. His ultimate goal is to build a building that would inspire people to worship and be drawn closer to God.

James, John, Simon and Thomas—Jesus disciples who are requested to leave behind firewood for the next group of travelers. They encounter a stranger who wants to see Jesus.

Philip—a disciple of John the Baptist who has been instructed by John to go and follow Jesus.

Andrew—a disciple of Jesus who was with Philip while following John the Baptist.

Matthew—a disciple of Jesus who was a former tax collector. He has a hard time fitting in with the group and clashes often with Simon. He finds encouragement in Phillip.

Mary & Rhema—the two women who are among the followers of

Jesus who have a desire to study the Torah.

Jesus—the leader of the group who invites Philip and Nathanael to become his disciple. Jesus opposes adding more structure to the group until after he is no longer present.

Summary of Season 2 Episode 2 I Saw You

The episode opens with Nathanael, a Jewish architect, trying to convince a Roman foreman that if he does not follow his requirements for the type of cement needed, the building structure will not be safe. The Roman takes Nathanael to be an arrogant Jew who is trying to give out orders regardless of what is going on at the site. Nathanael knows his future as an architect depends on the success of this first project. Because the proper instructions for cement from Nathanael are not followed, the building collapses, and so does his future along with it.

The next scene involves James, John, Simon, and Thomas cutting wood and putting it up for the next group of travelers who may be passing through. They are interrupted by a stranger who wants to see Jesus, but they are weary of him. The stranger is Philip, a former disciple of John the Baptist. John has sent Philip to follow Jesus, and Jesus invites him to become one of his disciples. Philip is the most mature spiritually of the disciples having previously spent considerable time with John the Baptist.

Philip is quick to pick up on the negative feelings Simon often directs at Matthew. Philip comes to Matthew's aid and encourages Matthew at various times throughout the episode. Matthew appreciates the presence of Philip in the group, and Philip's willingness to teach him new things. Matthew shares his past and present pain with Philip. Matthew discovers he does not have to allow others to define him by his past, especially those who are following Christ. One's confidence comes from the reality of being called by Jesus.

Nathanael tries to deal with his pain by visiting a bar. He shares his sorrow with the bartender. Nathanael had wanted to one day build synagogues throughout the country. He feels as though God had created him to be an architect, and now that is not going to happen. He later sits under a tree without a purpose. He feels alone and as though God has abandoned him. He burns the architectural plans that he had for a magnificent synagogue. As the plans burn, he cries out to God, "Do you see me?"

Later, Jesus encounters Philip at the campsite. Jesus remembers Philip from being with Andrew when Jesus was baptized by John. Philip tells Jesus that John had said he had met with a Pharisee while in prison. Philip is surprised to know that Jesus has a friend who is a Pharisee. Jesus informs Philip the group is heading to Caesarea Philippi in Syria next. Philip thinks that's a dangerous move and appears to be a death wish.

Mary and Rhema discuss the challenges of traveling with Jesus. They both want to know more of the Torah. Mary agrees to teach Rhema to read and to write. Matthew agrees to help them with the process. Thomas is a little jealous that Rhema didn't ask him for help.

Simon continues to make like difficult for Matthew. He objects to Matthew writing down the teachings of Jesus, because he thinks people could use the writings against him. Matthew simply wants an accurate account of the words that Jesus spoke. Matthew's note taking reminds Peter of the notes Matthew use to write about him in order to give it to the Romans. Simon informs Jesus of Matthew's note-taking, but is surprised to know that Jesus supports Matthew in his efforts.

Simon also wants more structure for the group to operate especially when Jesus is away for a couple of days. He volunteers to be in charge, but Jesus is not open to the idea yet. Jesus mentions one day he will no longer be with them, but that's a topic for another time. Peter asks if it will be soon, but Jesus replies that soon is not easy to define.

Once in Caesarea Philippi, a Roman city, Philip goes in search of his friend Nathanael. He finds Nathanael, and Nathanael shares his misfortune. Philip tells Nathanael about Jesus, but Nathanael rejects Jesus outright over the fact that he was from Nazareth. Philip encourages Nathanael to come and see. When Jesus engages Nathanael, Nathanael can't believe all the things that Jesus already knows about him. When Jesus says, "I saw you under the fig tree when you were at your lowest moment," Nathanael believes that Jesus is the Messiah. How could anyone have known everything Jesus knew about him.

Scriptures Woven Into Season 2 Episode 2 I Saw You

31 Do to others as you would have them do to you. *The New International Version* (Grand Rapids, MI: Zondervan, 2011), Lk 6:31.

13 When morning came, he called his disciples to him and chose twelve of them, whom he also designated apostles: 14 Simon (whom he named Peter), his brother Andrew, James, John, Philip, Bartholomew, 15 Matthew, Thomas, James son of Alphaeus, Simon who was called the Zealot, 16 Judas son of James, and Judas Iscariot, who became a traitor. *The New International Version* (Grand Rapids, MI: Zondervan, 2011), Lk 6:13–16.

35 The next day John was there again with two of his disciples. 36 When he saw Jesus passing by, he said, "Look, the Lamb of God!" 37 When the two disciples heard him say this, they followed Jesus. 38 Turning around, Jesus saw them following and asked, "What do you want?" They said, "Rabbi" (which means "Teacher"), "where are you staying?" 39 "Come," he replied, "and you will see."

So they went and saw where he was staying, and they spent that day with him. It was about four in the afternoon. 40 Andrew, Simon Peter's brother, was one of the two who heard what John had said and who had followed Jesus. 41 The first thing Andrew did was to find his brother Simon and tell him, "We have found the Messiah" (that is, the Christ). 42 And he brought him to Jesus. *The New International Version* (Grand Rapids, MI: Zondervan, 2011), Jn 1:35–42.

6 I will send fire on Magog and on those who live in safety in the coastlands, and they will know that I am the Lord. 7 " 'I will make known my holy name among my people Israel. I will no longer let my holy name be profaned, and the nations will know that I the Lord am the Holy One in Israel. 8 It is coming! It will surely take place, declares the Sovereign Lord. This is the day I have spoken of. 9 " 'Then those who live in the towns of Israel will go out and use the weapons for fuel and burn them up—the small and large shields, the bows and arrows, the war clubs and spears. For seven years they will use them for fuel. 10 They will not need to gather wood from the fields or cut it from the forests, because they will use the weapons for fuel. And they will plunder those who plundered them and loot those who looted them, declares the Sovereign Lord.
The New International Version (Grand Rapids, MI: Zondervan, 2011), Eze 39:6–10.

17 Therefore, if anyone is in Christ, the new creation has come: The old has gone, the new is here. *The New International Version* (Grand Rapids, MI: Zondervan, 2011), 2 Co 5:17.

16 You did not choose me, but I chose you and appointed you so that you might go and bear fruit—fruit that will last—and so that whatever you ask in my name the Father will give you.
The New International Version (Grand Rapids, MI: Zondervan, 2011), Jn 15:16.

1 Hear my prayer, Lord; let my cry for help come to you. 2 Do not hide your face from me when I am in distress. Turn your ear to me; when I call, answer me quickly. *The New International Version* (Grand Rapids, MI: Zondervan, 2011), Ps 102:1–2.

27 Jesus and his disciples went on to the villages around Caesarea Philippi. On the way he asked them, "Who do people say I am?" *The New International Version* (Grand Rapids, MI: Zondervan, 2011), Mk 8:27.

8 But do not forget this one thing, dear friends: With the Lord a day is like a thousand years, and a thousand years are like a day. 9 The Lord is not slow in keeping his promise, as some understand slowness. Instead he is patient with you, not wanting anyone to perish, but everyone to come to repentance. *The New International Version* (Grand Rapids, MI: Zondervan, 2011), 2 Pe 3:8–9.

15 The Lord your God will raise up for you a prophet like me from among you, from your fellow Israelites. You must listen to him. *The New International Version* (Grand Rapids, MI: Zondervan, 2011), Dt 18:15.

43 The next day Jesus decided to leave for Galilee. Finding Philip, he said to him, "Follow me." 44 Philip, like Andrew and Peter, was from the town of Bethsaida. 45 Philip found Nathanael and told him, "We have found the one Moses wrote about in the Law, and about whom the prophets also wrote—Jesus of Nazareth, the son of Joseph." 46 "Nazareth! Can anything good come from there?" Nathanael asked. "Come and see," said Philip. *The New International Version* (Grand Rapids, MI: Zondervan, 2011), Jn 1:43–46.

43 The next day Jesus decided to leave for Galilee. Finding Philip,

he said to him, "Follow me." 44 Philip, like Andrew and Peter, was from the town of Bethsaida. 45 Philip found Nathanael and told him, "We have found the one Moses wrote about in the Law, and about whom the prophets also wrote—Jesus of Nazareth, the son of Joseph." 46 "Nazareth! Can anything good come from there?" Nathanael asked. "Come and see," said Philip. 47 When Jesus saw Nathanael approaching, he said of him, "Here truly is an Israelite in whom there is no deceit." 48 "How do you know me?" Nathanael asked. Jesus answered, "I saw you while you were still under the fig tree before Philip called you." 49 Then Nathanael declared, "Rabbi, you are the Son of God; you are the king of Israel." 50 Jesus said, "You believe because I told you I saw you under the fig tree. You will see greater things than that." 51 He then added, "Very truly I tell you, you will see 'heaven open, and the angels of God ascending and descending on' the Son of Man."*The New International Version* (Grand Rapids, MI: Zondervan, 2011), Jn 1:43–51.

10 Jacob left Beersheba and set out for Harran. 11 When he reached a certain place, he stopped for the night because the sun had set. Taking one of the stones there, he put it under his head and lay down to sleep. 12 He had a dream in which he saw a stairway resting on the earth, with its top reaching to heaven, and the angels of God were ascending and descending on it.*The New International Version* (Grand Rapids, MI: Zondervan, 2011), Ge 28:10–12.

Biblical Characters Who Are Part Of Episode 2 I Saw You

Nathanael

Nathanael is an actual biblical character who meets Jesus in chapter 1 of the gospel of John. He is brought to Jesus by Philip ,and most of the conversation between Jesus and Nathanael is recorded in the Scriptures. He is listed among Jesus' disciples in John Chapter 21. Nathanael is never mentioned in Matthew, Mark, or Luke, but

Bartholomew is. John never mentions Bartholomew but does mention Nathanael. The argument is put forward that Bartholomew and Nathanael are one and the same person. There is nothing recorded in Scriptures about Nathanael being an architect or having a desire to build synagogues. These things are added simply to give depth and personality to the disciple of whom little is mentioned in Scripture.

James, John, Simon, Thaddeus, Matthew and Thomas

These are all disciples of Jesus, and they travel with Jesus. Very little of their actions in this episode are actually recorded in Scriptures.

Philip

Philip is an actual biblical character and was a disciple of John the Baptist before becoming a disciple of Jesus. He does have a relationship with Andrew and with Nathanael. He does bring Nathanael to come and see Jesus. Philip is listed in the gospels as one of the twelve apostles. Philip is mentioned many times in the gospels. Other than Philip bringing Nathanael to Jesus, the Scriptures do not record the conversations that Philip has with the other disciples, especially with Peter.

Mary Magdalene

Mary is an actual biblical character, and women did follow Jesus. The Scriptures do not record the conversations and actions of Mary presented in this episode.

Jesus

Jesus is an actual biblical character. He does lead the disciples on a trip to Caesarea Philippi. He does come from Nazareth. He does invite Philip to become one of his disciples. He does encounter Nathanael and their conversation is recorded in the Scriptures. The conversations Jesus has with Simon, Philip and the other disciples in this episode are not found in the Scriptures.

Bible Study Discussion Questions For Season 2 Episode 2 I Saw you.

1. When was there a time in your life in which you had a need and you felt as though God saw you at that very moment?

2. How do you think Nathanael felt when the building collapsed in the beginning? Have you ever had a similar experience?

3. Why are the disciples so suspicious of Philip upon his arrival?

4. What role, gift, or dimension does Philip bring to the group?

5. Why does the conflict between Simon and Matthew seem to be escalating?

6. Matthew said he felt the whole world was inside of a circle and he was alone outside the circle. Have you ever felt yourself in that position?

7. Why is it so important to allow people the chance to start over with their lives when they come to Christ?

8. Matthew's parents pushed him to succeed at an early age. At age 8 he was already skipping ahead because of his ability. How can we push our children to do things that actually lead them away from God?

9. What emotions are Nathanael experiencing as he sits under the tree?

10. Philip asks Matthew if it was hard to leave it all behind to follow Jesus? How would you answer that question for yourself?

11. Jesus commends Peter on his leadership abilities, but tells him he could be a little nicer. What would Jesus say to you about your interactions with other people?

12. Why do you think Philip is surprised to hear that Jesus has a friend who is a Pharisee?

13. Philip goes out of his way to help build up Matthew with encouragement. Who are you encouraging in this point of your life?

14. Why doesn't Rhema know how to read and write?

15. Are there any ways in which the church may hinder women from reaching their full potential in knowing God?

16. Why does Jesus offer to take the next shift in pushing the cart? How important is being a servant to others to you?

17. Do you believe that each of you in this bible study group has a purpose from God?

18. Which character in this episode is most like you at this point in your life?

19. What did you learn about Jesus in this episode?

3 RESOURCES FOR EPISODE 3 MATT. 4:24

Season 2 Episode 3 Matthew 4:24
37 Minutes Viewing Time

The Main Characters

Philip—the disciple who wants to instruct Matthew on how to grow in his faith and how to understand the Torah.

Matthew—the disciple who is eager to learn more of the Jewish law that he missed out on because of his service as a tax collector. He is constantly put on the spot because of his previous life-style.

James, John, Thaddeus, Big James—all disciples of Jesus who are trying to manage the long lines of people who are waiting to be healed by Jesus.

Mary & Rhema—the two women in the camp that are seeking to follow Jesus, but feel as though they should be doing more and growing faster in the Lord.

James—the disciple struggling with the sincerity of the faith of those being healed and is afraid to ask Jesus for his own healing.

Thomas—the disciple with the most questions for Jesus, such as why is Rome still in charge, why hasn't James been healed, and what's it like to lose your father early.

Mary the mother of Jesus—Jesus mother arrives, greets the group especially Philip and is introduced to Matthew. She shares her experience of Jesus' birth.

Simon & Andrew—the disciples of Jesus who are brothers and who

Big James and John—the disciples who comes to the defense of Matthew when Simon goes too far.

Jesus—The Son of God who comes into the camp exhausted from a long day of healing people. He's thankful for his mother.

Summary of Season 2 Episode 3 Matthew 4:24

This episode begins with a long line of people waiting for the chance to get to Jesus one on one so that they can be healed. The disciples have been assigned the role of crowd control and maintaining order. They are doing this in assigned shifts. Much of the setting takes place in the camp the disciples set up earlier during the morning after a four hour journey to their present location.

Philip continues his efforts to assist Matthew in growing in his faith by teaching him about the presence of God and which passage of Scripture to memorize first. As people leave the line, Matthew is busy trying to get testimonies from them of what Jesus did for them so that he can record them. Matthew passes on to Mary and Rhema, the words given to him by Philip.

The disciples gather around each other to share their views. John points out that they are becoming famous because Jesus is famous. Philip issues the warning that with fame comes persecution. They share their ideas of what they had imagined the Messiah would be like and what he would be doing when he arrived. Few of their pre-conceived ideas match Jesus and what is taking place.

Little James is ready for the day to be over because he questions the sincerity of the faith of many of the people. Would the people accept Jesus without the healings or do they only accept him because of the healing? Thomas asks James, why Jesus has not healed him. James suffers from a form of paralysis. James has wondered why Jesus has not brought it up, but has never asked Jesus about it.

Mary the mother of Jesus makes a surprise visit to the group.

She immediately offers to help out and assist with the cooking. Andrew starts a game about money which leads to a low-key attack on Matthew. The group shares different things they have gone through. Mary shares on what it was like to give birth to Jesus. She ended with saying, "he doesn't need me anymore" which makes her sad.

Even though it has gotten very late, Jesus refuses to send anyone away, so the disciples have more time with each other. They discuss losses from the past, their desire to be good students, and their attitude toward the Jewish laws and customs. Simon attacks Matthew over not being Jewish and betraying the people by working with the Romans. Andrew joins in the attack. John reminds Simon of his betrayal of them in his deal with the Romans. Peter justifies his actions but condemns Matthew, and insists that he will never forgive Matthew for what he has done. Big James lets Peter know he has gone too far and demands that he stand down. It looks as though the disciples might end up in a physical fight with each other as tempers flare up.

In the midst of this, Jesus comes into the camp out of the darkness totally exhausted from what he's been doing. He walks past them all simply saying good night, while breathing heavily. He goes to his tent somewhat discouraged. His mother follows him to assist him in taking off his cloak, and she washes his feet to provide him with a level of comfort. Jesus tells her, "what would I do without you!" The disciples are all left speechless.

Scriptures Referenced in Season 2 Episode 3 Matthew 4:24

24 News about him spread all over Syria, and people brought to him all who were ill with various diseases, those suffering severe pain, the demon-possessed, those having seizures, and the paralyzed; and he healed them *The New International Version* (Grand Rapids, MI: Zondervan, 2011), Mt 4:24.

Where can I go from your Spirit? Where can I flee from your presence? 8 If I go up to the heavens, you are there; if I make my bed in the depths, you are there. 9 If I rise on the wings of the dawn, if I settle on the far side of the sea, 10 even there your hand will guide me, your right hand will hold me fast. 11 If I say, "Surely the darkness will hide me and the light become night around me," 12 even the darkness will not be dark to you; the night will shine like the day, for darkness is as light to you. *The New International Version* (Grand Rapids, MI: Zondervan, 2011), Ps 139:7–12.

22 You will be hated by everyone because of me, but the one who stands firm to the end will be saved. 23 *The New International Version* (Grand Rapids, MI: Zondervan, 2011), Mt 10:22–23.

As Jesus went on from there, he saw a man named Matthew sitting at the tax collector's booth. "Follow me," he told him, and Matthew got up and followed him. 10 While Jesus was having dinner at Matthew's house, many tax collectors and sinners came and ate with him and his disciples. 11 When the Pharisees saw this, they asked his disciples, "Why does your teacher eat with tax collectors and sinners?" *The New International Version* (Grand Rapids, MI: Zondervan, 2011), Mt 9:9–11.

Biblical Characters Who Are Part Of Season 2 Episode 3

Matthew 4:24

James, John, Simon, Thaddeus, Matthew, Phillip, Andrew, Big James, Mary, Mary Magdalene, Jesus, and Thomas

This episode is unique in that it attempts to describe what a day must have been like for the disciples, and what types of conflicts they may have had due to the diversity of their backgrounds and former life-styles. The episode is built around Matthew 4:24 which speaks of people coming to Jesus to be healed. None of the conversations or actions depicted in this episode are actually recorded in the Scriptures with the exception being people were healed by Jesus. Although we know that some women traveled with Jesus, Rhema is not an actual biblical figure by name. One has to keep in mind that the Chosen is not a series that attempts a literal view of what is recorded in the Scriptures, but provides a framework to view the characters who are found in the Scriptures.

Bible Study Questions Season 2 Episode 3 Matthew 4:24

1. What physical healing have you either experienced or know about that you are convinced was done by God?

2. When you have thought about Jesus healing "all who were present", did you envision a crowd surrounding Jesus pressing in on him or an orderly line as was portrayed in the episode? Do you think an orderly line would have been possible? Why or Why not?

3. Is it comforting or frightening to know that you cannot go anywhere where God is not already there?

4. If you had of been one of Jesus first called disciples, how would you have handled the fame associated with being part of his inner circle?

5. Mary Magdalene says, "I think he is here because we can't be holy without him." What do you think it means for us to be holy in the eyes of God?

6. James is concerned that some people only believe in Jesus because Jesus has healed them, not because of who he is? Do we usually begin by telling people "who Jesus is" or by telling people "what Jesus can do for them?" Why?

7. What would you refuse to give up in order to receive all the money you would need to be considered rich? Why

8. After Matthew left his wealth behind, he said he felt better, but he didn't know if he was happy. Can you relate in any way to what he was saying?

9. When Mary, the mother of Jesus, was describing what it was like for her when Jesus was born, did anything in her words surprise you?

10. Why does anger over a loss in people's lives cause them to abandon God and sometimes even who they are as a person?

11. Why do we sometimes rebel against the rules that have been given to us in the Scriptures?

12. Thomas struggles with the predicament of the Jews under the Romans with them being God's chosen people. What exactly does God owe to a person that has been chosen by God for a particular task?

13. Do you think Simon and Andrew would have attacked Matthew with their words in the way they did if Jesus had of been present? Why or why not?

14. Simon says that he will never forgive Matthew. How do you think Matthew felt at that moment? If you would have been Matthew, what would you have said or done?

15. Why do you think Big James comes to Matthew's defense? Have you ever experienced someone coming to your aid in an attack on you? If so, what did it do for you?

16. Why does this group that Jesus has called turn against itself so quickly? How does this happen among believers today?

17. Do you think Jesus is aware of their conversation when he enters the camp? Why or Why not?

18. What do you think the disciples are feeling when all Jesus says is "good night" as he passes through them all?

19. Why do you think Jesus tells his mother, "What would I do without you?"

20. What was your biggest take away from this episode?

4 RESOURCES FOR EPISODE 4 PERFECT OPPORTUNITY

Season 2 Episode 4 The Perfect Opportunity

59 Minutes

Main Characters

Jesse—young boy injured in a tree accident who becomes the man at the pool of Bethesda seeking to be healed by the stirring of the waters. He is Simon the Zealot's brother.

Simon—young boy who grows up very close to his brother Jesse, but is greatly affected by the Roman's mistreatment of the Jews. He joins the zealots and trains to become an assassin.

Mary Magdalene—one of the women following Jesus.

Mary—the mother of Jesus who is with him to celebrate the Feast of The Tabernacle.

Mathew, Big James, John, Andrew, Thaddeus, Thomas, James, Simon—the disciples of Jesus that Jesus has called to join him and they build the booth for the Feast of Tabernacles.

Rhema—one of the women following Jesus with the disciples.

Rabbi Shmuel—one of the Pharisees seeking to build a following and who is convinced that Jesus is a false prophet.

Atticus—one of the elite Romans who is both an investigator for terrorists and special kind of a soldier skilled in preventing assassination attempts.

Summary of Season 2 Episode 4 The Perfect Opportunity

The episode begins with a young boy falling out of a tree which leaves him paralyzed. He unfortunately witnesses his mother dying in childbirth, yet the baby brother that is born becomes his delight in life. The two of them grow up very close to each other. Their names are Jesse and Simon. Simon witnesses the abuse of the Jews by the Romans and this leads to a change in the paths the two brothers travel in life. Both are waiting for the Messiah to come, but they have different views of what the Messiah's presence will mean for God's people. Simon goes off and joins the zealots to train to become an assassin. His brother goes to the pool of Bethesda, where he will spend years of his life believing if he can be the first to get into the pool when the waters are stirred, he will be healed.

The disciples are getting ready to celebrate the Feast of the Tabernacles. They are building a temporary dwelling to live in accordance with the Feast. The Jews are to live in booths for seven days in memory of the children of Israel spending forty years in the desert. Philip explains the process to Matthew since Matthew has been away from the Jewish tradition while serving as a tax collector.

Simon the Zealot finally reaches the point in his training in which he is given an assignment. He is to go to Jerusalem to assassinate a Roman official. He is told to either carry out his mission or never return. What Simon does not know is that a Roman by the name of Atticus is tracking his every move and has figured out Simon's plan and the date of the attack. Atticus' plan is to catch Simon in the midst of the attack and kill him on the spot.

Rabbi Shmuel has left Capernaum and is ready to launch his career in Jerusalem. He is in the city trying to build a following of his own. He starts to preach to the people in the market who are willing to listen to him. The process is more difficult than he thought it would be. Matthew spots him and lets Thomas and Nathanael know that Shmuel could cause trouble for Jesus.

Jesus shares a meal with all of the disciples. It is a time for them to ask him questions. The disciples are somewhat confused by a prophecy in Zechariah in which all nations will celebrate the Feast of Tabernacles. After the meal, Andrew and Simon informs Jesus that Rabbi Shmuel is in Jerusalem which could mean trouble. Jesus invites Andrew, Simon and Matthew to go with him to Jerusalem.

Simon the zealot and Jesus both have reactions when they pass Jews being crucified on the road leading into Jerusalem. They both enter the city with radically different purposes, and both go to the Pool of Bethesda at different times.

Simon the Zealot goes to visit his brother Jesse at the pool. It's been 25 years since the last time they met. Their reunion is bitter sweet. There is conflict over the two different paths that brothers have chosen. They exchange different views of what the Messiah will do when he comes. Jesse can sense that his brother is about to attempt something dangerous. They trade Scripture passages back and forth. Simon finally says that he will know the Messiah has come when he sees his brother standing on his own two feet.

Jesus goes to the pool with his disciples Simon, John and Matthew. They pass a group of Pharisees. Jesus spots Jesse and goes to him with the question, "do you want to be healed?" Jesus and Jesse have a conversation with each other that culminates in Jesse's healing. Jesus slips away and the Pharisees come to yell at Jesse for picking up his mat on the Sabbath.

Jesse goes looking for his brother Simon. Simon is actively involved in the assassination plot. Everyone is in place and have received the signal to go ahead. Simon accidentally sees his brother walking and looking for him. The distraction destroys the timing for the assassination plot. The would be accomplices run away, and Simon goes looking for Jesse. The brothers are reunited as they hug each other. Atticus is shocked, confused, and surprised that Simon does not even make an attempt to follow through with the assassination attempt knowing how the Zealots operate.

The episode ends with Jesus walking with the disciples away from Jerusalem. One disciple says to Jesus, "waiting thirty minutes would not have mattered to the man. Why did you heal him on the Sabbath?" Jesus answered, "Sometimes you have to stir up the water."

Special Note Concerning The Motivation For People Being At The Pool Of Bethesda In John Chapter 5.

Here a great number of disabled people used to lie—the blind, the lame, the paralyzed. The multitude of sick people lay underneath the five colonnades. In modern times similar gatherings have happened in Fatima and Lourdes. Many people make pilgrimages to these sites to receive the healing benefit of the waters. The colonnade in Jerusalem was a place of collected human suffering—people attracted by a faint hope of being healed. To this place Jesus was also attracted, offering with his presence the kind of healing that went beyond the physical needs of the disabled. Waiting for the moving of the water. For an angel went down at a certain time into the pool and stirred up the water; then whoever stepped in first, after the stirring of the water, was made well of whatever disease he had. It is very doubtful this portion was written by John, since it is not found in the earliest manuscripts, and where it does occur in later manuscripts, it is often marked in such a way as to show that it is an addition. The passage was probably inserted later by scribes who felt it necessary to provide an explanation for the gathering of disabled people and the stirring of the water mentioned in verse 7. It is unclear whether an angel actually disturbed the water, or if this was just a local superstition used to explain the natural movement in a pool of water fed by a spring. But somehow the waters were stirred and seemed to have had curative powers.Bruce B. Barton, *John*, Life Application Bible Commentary (Wheaton, IL: Tyndale House, 1993), 99–100.

Scriptures Woven Into Episode 4 The Perfect Opportunity

33 The Lord said to Moses, 34 "Say to the Israelites: 'On the fifteenth day of the seventh month the Lord's Festival of Tabernacles begins, and it lasts for seven days. 35 The first day is a sacred assembly; do no regular work. 36 For seven days present food offerings to the Lord, and on the eighth day hold a sacred assembly and present a food offering to the Lord. It is the closing special assembly; do no regular work. *The New International Version* (Grand Rapids, MI: Zondervan, 2011), Le 23:33–36.

39 " 'So beginning with the fifteenth day of the seventh month, after you have gathered the crops of the land, celebrate the festival to the Lord for seven days; the first day is a day of sabbath rest, and the eighth day also is a day of sabbath rest. 40 On the first day you are to take branches from luxuriant trees—from palms, willows and other leafy trees—and rejoice before the Lord your God for seven days. 41 Celebrate this as a festival to the Lord for seven days each year. This is to be a lasting ordinance for the generations to come; celebrate it in the seventh month. 42 Live in temporary shelters for seven days: All native-born Israelites are to live in such shelters 43 so your descendants will know that I had the Israelites live in temporary shelters when I brought them out of Egypt. I am the Lord your God.' " *The New International Version* (Grand Rapids, MI: Zondervan, 2011), Le 23:39–43.

16 Then the survivors from all the nations that have attacked Jerusalem will go up year after year to worship the King, the Lord Almighty, and to celebrate the Festival of Tabernacles. 17 If any of

the peoples of the earth do not go up to Jerusalem to worship the King, the Lord Almighty, they will have no rain. 18 If the Egyptian people do not go up and take part, they will have no rain. The Lord will bring on them the plague he inflicts on the nations that do not go up to celebrate the Festival of Tabernacles. 19 This will be the punishment of Egypt and the punishment of all the nations that do not go up to celebrate the Festival of Tabernacles

The New International Version (Grand Rapids, MI: Zondervan, 2011), Zec 14:16–19.

16 Three times a year all your men must appear before the Lord your God at the place he will choose: at the Festival of Unleavened Bread, the Festival of Weeks and the Festival of Tabernacles. No one should appear before the Lord empty-handed: 17 Each of you must bring a gift in proportion to the way the Lord your God has blessed you. *The New International Version* (Grand Rapids, MI: Zondervan, 2011), Dt 16:16–17.

17 The Lord your God is with you, the Mighty Warrior who saves. He will take great delight in you; in his love he will no longer rebuke you, but will rejoice over you with singing." *The New International Version* (Grand Rapids, MI: Zondervan, 2011), Zep 3:17.

19 At that time I will deal with all who oppressed you. I will rescue the lame; I will gather the exiles. I will give them praise and honor in every land where they have suffered shame. *The New International Version* (Grand Rapids, MI: Zondervan, 2011), Zep 3:19.

There is a time for everything, and a season for every activity under the heavens: 2 a time to be born and a time to die, a time to plant and a time to uproot, 3 a time to kill and a time to heal, a time to tear down and a time to build, *The New International Version* (Grand

Rapids, MI: Zondervan, 2011), Ec 3:1–3.

Some time later, Jesus went up to Jerusalem for one of the Jewish festivals. 2 Now there is in Jerusalem near the Sheep Gate a pool, which in Aramaic is called Bethesda and which is surrounded by five covered colonnades. 3 Here a great number of disabled people used to lie—the blind, the lame, the paralyzed. [4] 5 One who was there had been an invalid for thirty-eight years. 6 When Jesus saw him lying there and learned that he had been in this condition for a long time, he asked him, "Do you want to get well?" 7 "Sir," the invalid replied, "I have no one to help me into the pool when the water is stirred. While I am trying to get in, someone else goes down ahead of me." 8 Then Jesus said to him, "Get up! Pick up your mat and walk." 9 At once the man was cured; he picked up his mat and walked. The day on which this took place was a Sabbath, 10 and so the Jewish leaders said to the man who had been healed, "It is the Sabbath; the law forbids you to carry your mat." 11 But he replied, "The man who made me well said to me, 'Pick up your mat and walk.' " 12 So they asked him, "Who is this fellow who told you to pick it up and walk?" 13 The man who was healed had no idea who it was, for Jesus had slipped away into the crowd that was there. *The New International Version* (Grand Rapids, MI: Zondervan, 2011), Jn 5:1–13.

5 After this there was a feast of the Jews; and Jesus went up to Jerusalem. 2 Now there is at Jerusalem by the sheep market a pool, which is called in the Hebrew tongue Bethesda, having five porches. 3 In these lay a great multitude of impotent folk, of blind, halt, withered, waiting for the moving of the water. 4 For an angel went down at a certain season into the pool, and troubled the water: whosoever then first after the troubling of the water stepped in was made whole of whatsoever disease he had. 5 And a certain man was there, which had an infirmity thirty and eight years. 6 When Jesus saw him lie, and knew that he had been now a long time in that case,

he saith unto him, Wilt thou be made whole? 7 The impotent man answered him, Sir, I have no man, when the water is troubled, to put me into the pool: but while I am coming, another steppeth down before me. 8 Jesus saith unto him, Rise, take up thy bed, and walk *The Holy Bible: King James Version*, Electronic Edition of the 1900 Authorized Version. (Bellingham, WA: Logos Research Systems, Inc., 2009), Jn 5.

Biblical Characters Who Are Part Of Season2 Episode 4

The Perfect Opportunity

The Man Who Was Lame

The Scriptures indicate there was a man who was lame and had been at the pool of Bethesda for 38 years. He did encounter Jesus and was healed by Jesus. He was challenged by the Pharisees. The Scriptures do not record the man's name as being Jesse, nor does it record any of the drama concerning him other than his conversations with Jesus and the Pharisees. His story can be found in John's gospel chapter 5.

Mary, Mary Magdalene, Simon, Andrew, Phillip, Big James, John, Thomas, Thaddeus and Nathanael

These are all actual biblical characters in this episode, but the Scriptures do not record anything about their involvement with the Feast of Tabernacles. So most of their conversation has been created to add depth to the characters. They do accurately speak truth concerning the meaning of the Festival of Tabernacles. The Scriptures do not record any of the disciples being present with Jesus at the time of the healing of the man at the pool of Bethesda.

Jesus

The Scriptures do record Jesus going to Jerusalem for one of the Jewish festivals and while he is there he does go to the pool of Bethesda where there is a lame man. The man has been there for thirty-eight years and he does have a conversation with Jesus, prior to Jesus healing him. Jesus does sneak away from the man before he recognizes that it was Jesus who healed him. The Jewish leaders do get upset with Jesus over his healing on the Sabbath?

Bible Study Discussion Questions Season 2 Episode 4

1. When was a time you happened to be in the right place at the right time and it made a course correction or change in your life?

2. What impressed you about the relationship between Jesse and Simon in their early lives?

3. Why do you think Simon made the decision to join the Zealots? Have you ever witnessed an injustice that caused you to see things differently?

4. What do you think it means when the Scriptures speaks of God being on the side of the oppressed?

5. Do you think Jesse handled his situation of being lame in an appropriate manner? Why or why not?

6. Simon had a confident plan, but his life was in danger without him knowing it from the Roman Atticus? When has there been a time when your life was in danger, but you were not aware of it, but God's grace was there for you?

7. Why do you think the disciples struggled with the prophecy in Zephaniah that other nations would be invited to celebrate the Festival of Tabernacles?

8. What's the possible danger of seeing ourselves as God's chosen people or our nation as God's chosen nation?

9. What did you learn from Jesse's and Simon's conversation at the pool of Bethesda? Which of the two could you identify with more easily?

10. On his way to Jerusalem, there was a scene in which Jesus looked at some men being crucified and time seemed to have

slowed down? If you had been Jesus at that moment, what do you think would have been going through your mind?

11. Why do you think Jesus only went to the pool of Bethesda for Jesse when there were clearly many other people who needed a miracle present at the pool? Is God always fair in his treatment of others?

12. Why does Jesus ask Jesse, "Do you want to get well?"

13. What can we learn from Jesus' approach to Jesse in relating to other people who appear to have a need in their lives?

14. Jesse responds to Jesus' question with excuses. How do excuses keep us from experiencing the life God may want us to have?

15. Several times in the episode, there is mention that the stirring of the waters is rooted in pagan idolatry. Why on earth would

Jesus go to such a place since it wasn't rooted in sound theology? What are the implications for us today?

16. Was Jesus looking for controversy when he told the man to pick up his mat and walk while knowing it was the Sabbath day?

17. When should followers of Christ shy away from conflict and when should they put themselves in the place to challenge the status quo?

18. What part of this episode was the most meaningful to you?

5 RESOURCES FOR EPISODE 5 SPIRIT

Season 2 Episode 5 Spirit
48 Minutes Viewing Time

The Main Characters

Mary Magdalene—While picking fruit out alone, a Roman soldier approaches Mary on horseback. She hides, but the experience causes her to flashback to a time when she was abused by some Romans soldiers. She will have additional flashbacks in this episode.

Shmuel—Pharisee and rabbi who interrogates Jesse over the healing at the pool of Bethesda and organizer of a political maneuver to get the Sanhedrin to take his claims against Jesus seriously.

Jesse—the man Jesus healed at the pool of Bethesda who is interrogated by the Pharisees and later deceptively questioned by a Roman agent.

Atticus—the Roman agent who is still searching for Simon the Zealot, and he questions Jesse about his healing. He follows the trail of Simon throughout the episode.

Simon the Zealot—the brother of Jesse, who first encounters a man possessed by demons. Eventually he receives an invitation from Jesus to join him as a disciple.

John the Baptist—Jesus' cousin who prepared the way for Jesus. He wonders what's taking Jesus so long to launch his ministry, and he is determined to go to Jerusalem to challenge Herod's choice of a new wife.

Rhema—one of the women following Jesus who is being taught how to read by Mary Magdalene.

Thomas and Matthew—two of Jesus' disciples who have a lot in common talent wise, and it causes them friction in getting along with each other.

Jesus—The Son of Man has serious talks with John The Baptist, sets a demonic free, and calls Simon the Zealot to join his group of disciples.

Man possessed by demon—a man possessed by a demon threatens to physically attack some of the disciples and has the demons cast out by Jesus, but not before the demons have an affect on Mary Magdalene.

Simon—disciple of Jesus and Andrew's brother. He notices that Mary is missing from the group. Jesus sends Simon and Matthew to go and find Mary.

Summary of Season 2 Episode 5 Spirit

The episode begins with Mary Magdalene picking fruit as she recites portions of Psalm 139. She sees a Roman soldier approaching on horseback, and she hides to keep from being seen. The sight of the soldier causes her to experience a flashback from Season One of the Chosen in which it was shown she had been sexually abused by some Roman soldiers.

The Pharisees are trying their best to discredit Jesus. They question Jesse, the man Jesus had healed in the previous episode at the pool of Bethesda. The Pharisees have some severe issues with Jesus telling him to pick up his mat on the Sabbath. Jesse is more interested in talking about his healing than he is breaking the Sabbath. Later in the episode, the Pharisee Shmuel will try a political maneuver to reopen a case that Nicodemus had gotten closed. He looks for allies that will help him to find Jesus and to charge him with false prophecy.

Atticus is the Roman agent who was prepared to kill Simon the Zealot (Jesse' brother) in the previous episode. When Jesse leaves the interrogation by the Pharisees, Atticus engages Jesse on the miracle Jesse experienced, but his ultimate motive is to find out some information on Simon the Zealot as well as on Jesus. Atticus will appear hiding throughout the episode spying on people.

Simon the Zealot is shown practicing his art of fighting. He wants to be ready to join the Messiah's army. He is approached by a man possessed by a demon. The man wants Simon to kill him and end his misery, but Simon refuses because the man is neither a Roman or tax collector. The demons inside the man does recognize there is something holy about Simon.

Jesus and the disciples run into John The Baptist while they are walking on a trail. John lets them know that he is going to Jerusalem to call out Herod for marrying his brother's wife. Jesus and John will have conversations on their perspective roles in the kingdom. John thinks Jesus should be revealing himself much quicker than he is. They differ on what should be their priorities. Jesus warns John to be careful with his decision to go and confront Herod. John wants Jesus to be more confrontational and to spend less time going off by himself. By the end of their conversations in this episode, it is obvious the two have a great love and respect for each other.

Mary is giving reading lessons to Rhema, but Mary is distracted. She's still being affected by her earlier flashback in that she is both anxious and nervous. Thomas and Matthew engage each other, and Matthew notices the interactions with Mary and Rhema are not going well. Thomas is jealous that Matthew may have a romantic interest in Rhema. Mary starts to hear voices in her head. Pretty soon Thomas, Matthew and Rhema also hear the wild cries. The cries are coming from the man that Simon the Zealot ran into earlier.

The man who was possessed by the demons shows up at the camp and calls Mary by the name "Lillith." Lillith was the name Mary went by when she was possessed by the demons. Mary attempts to get the man to say what his real name is, but the demon won't allow it. The demon launches an attack but is stalled first by Simon the Zealot. Jesus and the other disciples arrive on the scene, and Jesus casts the demon out of the man. The man's name is Caleb. Mary sneaks away from the group as Jesus completes Caleb's healing.

Jesus introduces Simon the Zealot to Simon and the other disciples. Jesus takes Simon the Zealot alone for a walk and explains to him what it means for his followers to be his disciple. Simon is ready to die and fight for Jesus, but Jesus is calling for something different. Jesus takes Simon's secret dagger and throws it into the water. Meanwhile Atticus is spying on the two of them and trying to make sense of Jesus throwing the dagger into the water.

Mary is on her way to the nearby town crying and confused. When another Roman soldier comes up behind her on horseback, her flash back is relived of her earlier life before Jesus. She heads for a tavern similar to where Jesus first found her in Season 1.

John The Baptist and Jesus share touching moments as John heads for the road leading to Jerusalem. Jesus lets John know, that very soon Jesus will reveal himself to others. He again warns John to be careful.

Simon shares anecdotes about each disciple to Simon the Zealot to welcome him in the group. Simon notices that Mary is missing and tells Jesus. Jesus sends Simon and Matthew to town to find Mary.

Scriptures Women Into Season 2 Episode 5 Spirit

7 Where can I go from your Spirit? Where can I flee from your presence? 8 If I go up to the heavens, you are there; if I make my bed in the depths, you are there. 9 If I rise on the wings of the dawn, if I settle on the far side of the sea, 10 even there your hand will guide me, your right hand will hold me fast. 11 If I say, "Surely the darkness will hide me and the light become night around me," 12 even the darkness will not be dark to you; the night will shine like the day, for darkness is as light to you. *The New International Version* (Grand Rapids, MI: Zondervan, 2011), Ps 139:7–12.

5 Some time later, Jesus went up to Jerusalem for one of the Jewish festivals. 2 Now there is in Jerusalem near the Sheep Gate a pool, which in Aramaic is called Bethesda and which is surrounded by five covered colonnades. 3 Here a great number of disabled people used to lie—the blind, the lame, the paralyzed. [4] 5 One who was there had been an invalid for thirty-eight years. 6 When Jesus saw him lying there and learned that he had been in this condition for a long time, he asked him, "Do you want to get well?" 7 "Sir," the invalid replied, "I have no one to help me into the pool when the water is stirred. While I am trying to get in, someone else goes down ahead of me." 8 Then Jesus said to him, "Get up! Pick up your mat and walk." 9 At once the man was cured; he picked up his mat and walked. The day on which this took place was a Sabbath, 10 and so the Jewish leaders said to the man who had been healed, "It is the Sabbath; the law forbids

you to carry your mat." 11 But he replied, "The man who made me well said to me, 'Pick up your mat and walk.' " 12 So they asked him, "Who is this fellow who told you to pick it up and walk?" 13 The man who was healed had no idea who it was, for Jesus had slipped away into the crowd that was there. 14 Later Jesus found him at the temple and said to him, "See, you are well again. Stop sinning or something worse may happen to you." 15 The man went away and told the Jewish leaders that it was Jesus who had made him well. *The New International Version* (Grand Rapids, MI: Zondervan, 2011), Jn 5:1–15.

5 Some time later, Jesus went up to Jerusalem for one of the Jewish festivals. 2 Now there is in Jerusalem near the Sheep Gate a pool, which in Aramaic is called Bethesda and which is surrounded by five covered colonnades. 3 Here a great number of disabled people used to lie—the blind, the lame, the paralyzed. [4] 5 One who was there had been an invalid for thirty-eight years. 6 When Jesus saw him lying there and learned that he had been in this condition for a long time, he asked him, "Do you want to get well?" 7 "Sir," the invalid replied, "I have no one to help me into the pool when the water is stirred. While I am trying to get in, someone else goes down ahead of me." 8 Then Jesus said to him, "Get up! Pick up your mat and walk." 9 At once the man was cured; he picked up his mat and walked. The day on which this took place was a Sabbath, 10 and so the Jewish leaders said to the man who had been healed, "It is the Sabbath; the law forbids you to carry your mat." 11 But he replied, "The man who made me well said to me, 'Pick up your mat and walk.' " 12 So they asked him, "Who is this fellow who told you to pick it up and walk?" 13 The man who was healed had no idea who it was, for Jesus had slipped away into the crowd that was there. 14 Later Jesus found him at the temple and

said to him, "See, you are well again. Stop sinning or something worse may happen to you." 15 The man went away and told the Jewish leaders that it was Jesus who had made him well. *The New International Version* (Grand Rapids, MI: Zondervan, 2011), Jn 5:1–15.

When morning came, he called his disciples to him and chose twelve of them, whom he also designated apostles: 14 Simon (whom he named Peter), his brother Andrew, James, John, Philip, Bartholomew, 15 Matthew, Thomas, James son of Alphaeus, Simon who was called the Zealot, 16 Judas son of James, and Judas Iscariot, who became a traitor. *The New International Version* (Grand Rapids, MI: Zondervan, 2011), Lk 6:13–16.

11 Truly I tell you, among those born of women there has not risen anyone greater than John the Baptist; yet whoever is least in the kingdom of heaven is greater than he. 12 From the days of John the Baptist until now, the kingdom of heaven has been subjected to violence, and violent people have been raiding it. 13 For all the Prophets and the Law prophesied until John. 14 And if you are willing to accept it, he is the Elijah who was to come. 15 Whoever has ears, let them hear. 16 "To what can I compare this generation? They are like children sitting in the marketplaces and calling out to others: 17 " 'We played the pipe for you, and you did not dance; we sang a dirge, and you did not mourn.' 18 For John came neither eating nor drinking, and they say, 'He has a demon.' 19 The Son of Man came eating and drinking, and they say, 'Here is a glutton and a drunkard, a friend of tax collectors and sinners.' But wisdom is proved right by her deeds."*The New International Version* (Grand Rapids, MI: Zondervan, 2011), Mt 11:11–19.

17 For Herod himself had given orders to have John arrested,

and he had him bound and put in prison. He did this because of Herodias, his brother Philip's wife, whom he had married. 18 For John had been saying to Herod, "It is not lawful for you to have your brother's wife." 19 So Herodias nursed a grudge against John and wanted to kill him. But she was not able to, 20 because Herod feared John and protected him, knowing him to be a righteous and holy man. When Herod heard John, he was greatly puzzled; yet he liked to listen to him. *The New International Version* (Grand Rapids, MI: Zondervan, 2011), Mk 6:17–20.

Biblical Characters Who Are A Part Of Season 2 Episode 5 Spirit

Mary Magdalene

Mary Magdalene is an actual biblical character, but the Scriptures do not record any of the events that take place in this episode. Mary is recorded in the in the Scriptures by Matthew, Mark, Luke and John as being one of the first to whom Jesus appeared after the resurrection. She is mentioned as being present at the crucifixion of Jesus. There is nothing in Scripture to suggests Mary Magdalene turned back to her former life-style for a time.

Jesse

There is an actual biblical character that was healed by Jesus at the pool of Bethesda, however the Bible never states what his name was. He was interrogated by the Pharisees and the words that he said Jesus told him are recorded in the scriptures in John Chapter Five. The Scriptures do not record him as being the brother of Simon the Zealot.

Simon the Zealot

There is a biblical character named Simon the Zealot, and he is listed in all of the gospels as one of the twelve disciples called by Jesus. We know nothing of his personal life in the Scriptures. The episode does show what a zealot was like and why they received the name. None of the actions in this episode done by Simon the Zealot are recorded in the Scriptures other than he did become one of the twelve.

Caleb-The Man Possessed
There are several mentions in Scriptures of men who are possessed by demons who cut themselves, have unusual strength, and cry out in anguish. The Scriptures do not record any of their names. Jesus does cast demons out of several people, but this particular casting out in this setting is not recorded in Scriptures.

John The Baptist
John the Baptist is an actual biblical character, and he is the cousin of Jesus. He does go to confront Herod about his marriage to his brother's wife. John did wonder why Jesus was taking so long to manifest himself during the time John was in prison. The conversations between John and Jesus are very interesting and could have very well taken place, but they are not recorded in the Scripture. He and Jesus do have different approaches to preaching and the way in which they relate to others.

Thomas, Matthew, Simon
They are all disciples of Jesus recorded in the Scriptures. However none of the scenes they are in in this episode are recorded in the Scriptures. We are given some insights into some of the kinds of conflicts the disciples may have had with each other. There is no foundation in Scripture for Jesus sending Simon and Matthew into town to find Mary.

Bible Study Discussion Questions Season 2 Episode 5
Spirit

1. When have you had an experience of something that immediately caused a flashback for you either good or bad?

2. Why do you think Pharisee Shmuel and the others gave Jesse such a hard time over his healing by Jesus?

3. Do you think Jesse was naïve in sharing his testimony with the Roman Atticus? How can we know when it's wise to share our testimony, and when it's better to keep it quiet for the moment?

4. Do you view Simon the Zealot as a terrorist, or as a person trying to live a dedicated life to God? Why?

5. Do you think people can still be possessed by demons today or did that end with the time of Jesus and the apostles? Why?

6. If you would have been Simon, how would you have responded to the man's request to please kill him so that he could be free of the demon's influence?

7. John the Baptist said someone needed to call Herod out on what he did in marrying his brother's wife, and he was going to Jerusalem to tell him he was wrong? How do we know when to call people out for their sin, and when to just keep preaching the gospel.

8. When it comes to those who are non-believers, what's the standard of righteousness we should try to hold them accountable to?

9. John the Baptist accuses Jesus of avoiding specific pronouncements on a number of things? Do you think it would have been more helpful if Jesus had given us more commandments on what not to do? Why?

10. In earlier episodes, the disciples wanted Jesus to hurry to declare himself as the Messiah as soon as possible. John likewise wants Jesus to hurry up and make a public declaration. Why are we more anxious about God doing something, than God seems to be?

11. Jesus told Simon the Zealot that he healed Jesse, in order to get Simon's attention. Have you ever taken notice of God because of something God did in someone else's life?

12. Jesus told Simon the Zealot, "no one buys their way into our group by special skills." Why does God not need our special skills when he calls us into the kingdom?

13. Simon the Zealot found out that Jesus was very different from what he had imagined he would be. How have you found Jesus to be different from what you thought walking with him would be?

14. Jesus and John the Baptist have a very emotional farewell with each other. What do you think was going through Jesus' mind as he saw John walking away down the road headed for Jerusalem?

15. Do you think John the Baptist was following God's will for his life as he headed toward Jerusalem? Why or Why not?

16. When have you thought you were doing God's will, but it ended up costing you a terrible price?

17. Why do you think Mary didn't try to talk to Jesus before leaving the group?

18. What keeps us from talking to Jesus at times when we are troubled?

19. Where do you see the love of Jesus most clearly displayed in this episode?

6 RESOURCES FOR EPISODE 6 UNLAWFUL

Season 2 Episode 6 Unlawful

44 Minutes Viewing Time

Main Characters

Ahimelek—the priest who explains the Bread of the Presence and gives David bread for him and his men.

David—the young man who comes to Ahimelek to ask for any food that may be available.

Simon—the disciple of Jesus given the task to find Mary Magdalene.

Matthew—the disciple of Jesus also given the task to enter the city and find Mary Magdalene.

Mary Magdalene—the woman disciple who has left Jesus and returned to her former life.

Rhema and Mary—the women who are searching for different types of plants to eat.

Thomas—the disciple in charge of the food supply who is worried they will not have enough to eat.

Shmuel—the Pharisee working to get charges against Jesus.

Simon the Zealot—the disciple who wants to organize a prison breakout for John The Baptist.

Andrew—the disciple who takes the news of John's imprisonment the hardest.

Jesus—the one who forgives Mary, heals a man with a withered hand and demonstrates his lordship over the Sabbath.

Elam—the man with the withered hand

Summary Of Episode 6 Unlawful

The episode begins with a scene from the Old Testament. Ahimelek the priest is explaining to his son the meaning behind the Bread of The Presence. David is fleeing from Saul, and he comes to request food from Ahimelek. David lies about the circumstances as to why he was requesting aid. After asking a few questions, Ahimelek turns over the Bread of the Presence to David so that he and his men could have food. He does not know that David has lied to him about everything.

The scene shifts to Simon and Matthew in a stable where they have spent the night in the town of Jericho. They have some conflict among themselves, but they do go about their task of searching for Mary Magdalene. Simon wants to be in charge of the search.

Mary, Jesus' mother, and Rhema go out looking for plants to eat. Rhema is surprised that Mary knew so much about which plants could be eaten and which could not. Mary explained that she had been poor almost all her life so her knowledge was a necessity. Rhema is disappointed that Jesus sent Simon and Matthew to find Mary Magdalene, knowing the two of them did not get along well. She asks, "What benefit could come from using Mary Magdalene's pain to draw the two of them together?" Mary reminds her that they needed to trust God.

Mary is in a tavern gambling. She is winning and drinking

heavily. She decides she wants to take her winnings and leave, but the guy who has lost money to her demands the opportunity to win it back. When she says no, the guy gets up to go and fight her. Fortunately the bar tender intervenes. Mary then has a flashback to her childhood because of the fear that overcomes her. She sees her father asking her as a little girl, what do we do when we are afraid. She remembers Isaiah 43:1 and runs out the tavern leaving her winnings on the table.

Thomas is very nervous that they will run out of food before they reach their next destination. He doesn't understand why Jesus will not simply manufacture food out of thin air. Andrew lets him know, when he was a follower of John the Baptist, they would go days without food.

Big James and John are also worried about Mary Magdalene and even more so because of who Jesus sent to find her. James admit that he doesn't understand a lot about Jesus. John shares with his brother that he had wanted at one time to join the Zealots, but lacked the discipline required for all the physical exercises in the morning.

When Simon and Matthew enter a tavern searching for Mary, Simon wants to play the role of a tough guy to get some answers, but Matthew simply asks for help. As they leave the tavern, Matthew thinks the best course of action is for them to split up so they can cover more ground. Simon finally agrees. But then something unplanned happened.

Simon and Matthew are actually spotted by Mary, and she calls out to them. She is convinced that she could never return to Jesus with them. Jesus had already fixed her once, and she didn't believe she had the right to ask him to do it again.

Matthew points out to her what a difference she has made in his life and in Rhema's life. Simon follows his lead by reminding Mary of the difference she has made on several occasions helping others. They convince her that Jesus had called her for a reason. He was the one that sent them after her.

Meanwhile the Pharisee Shmuel is trying to get an audience to bring charges against Jesus. He is told that he has a very weak case and lacks the proper number of witnesses. He discovers he will not be able to make a case against Jesus purely on violations of the Torah. He will have to find a way to pit one religious group against another one to have his case heard.

Mary Magdalene does return to the camp with Simon and Matthew. They receive the news that John the Baptist has been arrested and placed in a heavily guarded prison. Mary, the mother of Jesus, takes Mary Magdalene to the tent Jesus is in. Jesus tells her that its good to have her back. Mary confesses how she regrets throwing everything away after all Jesus had done for her. Jesus lets her know that his redemption would not have been much of a redemption if it could be lost in a day. Jesus forgives her and they embrace each other. Matthew is listening to their conversation outside the tent.

Andrew takes John the Baptist's arrest the hardest, especially when he hears John has been sentenced to life in prison. Simon the Zealot is eager to organize his friends to try and break John out of prison. Phillip reminds him that he's a part of a New Order now, and breaking John out of prison is not an option.

Thomas informs Jesus of the food supply. Jesus' response is for them to talk to the Father about their need because they are going to leave in the morning. They visit a synagogue out in the middle of nowhere. The rabbi is preaching a message on who is not allowed to go into the temple.

There is a man sitting in the synagogue named Elam who has a withered hand. Jesus presents the question, "is it lawful to heal on the Sabbath?" By healing Elam, Jesus outrages the two rabbis. They kick Jesus and the others out of the synagogue. Jesus causes more trouble when he gives the disciples permission to eat some of the grain they were passing on the Sabbath. Jesus declares that the Son of Man is Lord of the Sabbath. The two rabbis feel compelled to report Jesus to higher authorities in order for justice to take place.

Scriptures Woven Into Season 2 Episode 6 Unlawful

10 "All who are skilled among you are to come and make everything the Lord has commanded: 11 the tabernacle with its tent and its covering, clasps, frames, crossbars, posts and bases; 12 the ark with its poles and the atonement cover and the curtain that shields it; 13 the table with its poles and all its articles and the bread of the Presence; *The New International Version* (Grand Rapids, MI: Zondervan, 2011), Ex 35:10–13.

David went to Nob, to Ahimelek the priest. Ahimelek trembled when he met him, and asked, "Why are you alone? Why is no one with you?" 2 David answered Ahimelek the priest, "The king sent me on a mission and said to me, 'No one is to know anything about the mission I am sending you on.' As for my men, I have told them to meet me at a certain place. 3 Now then, what do you have on hand? Give me five loaves of bread, or whatever you can find." 4 But the priest answered David, "I don't have any ordinary bread on hand; however, there is some consecrated bread here—provided the men have kept themselves from women." 5 David replied, "Indeed women have been kept from us, as usual whenever I set out. The men's bodies are holy even on missions that are not holy. How much more so today!" 6 So the priest gave him the consecrated bread, since there was no bread there except the bread of the Presence that had been removed from before the Lord and replaced by hot bread on the day it was taken away. *The New International Version* (Grand Rapids, MI: Zondervan, 2011), 1 Sa 21:1–6.

6 Now this I know: The Lord gives victory to his anointed. He answers him from his heavenly sanctuary with the victorious power of his right hand. 7 Some trust in chariots and some in horses, but we trust in the name of the Lord our God. 8 They are brought to their knees and fall, *The New International Version* (Grand Rapids, MI: Zondervan, 2011), Ps 20:6–8.

"Do not fear, for I have redeemed you; I have summoned you by name; you are mine. 2 When you pass through the waters, I will be with you; and when you pass through the rivers, they will not sweep over you. When you walk through the fire, you will not be burned;

the flames will not set you ablaze. 3 For I am the Lord your God, the Holy One of Israel, your Savior; *The New International Version* (Grand Rapids, MI: Zondervan, 2011), Is 43:1–3.

7 The law of the Lord is perfect, refreshing the soul. The statutes of the Lord are trustworthy, making wise the simple. 8 The precepts of the Lord are right, giving joy to the heart. The commands of the Lord are radiant, giving light to the eyes. 9 The fear of the Lord is pure, enduring forever. The decrees of the Lord are firm, and all of them are righteous. 10 They are more precious than gold, than much pure gold; they are sweeter than honey, than honey from the honeycomb. *The New International Version* (Grand Rapids, MI: Zondervan, 2011), Ps 19:7–10.

3 Now Herod had arrested John and bound him and put him in prison because of Herodias, his brother Philip's wife, 4 for John had been saying to him: "It is not lawful for you to have her." 5 Herod wanted to kill John, but he was afraid of the people, because they considered John a prophet. *The New International Version* (Grand Rapids, MI: Zondervan, 2011), Mt 14:3–5.

3 No Ammonite or Moabite or any of their descendants may enter the assembly of the Lord, not even in the tenth generation. 4 For they did not come to meet you with bread and water on your way when you came out of Egypt, and they hired Balaam son of Beor from Pethor in Aram Naharaim to pronounce a curse on you. 5 However, the Lord your God would not listen to Balaam but turned the curse into a blessing for you, because the Lord your God loves you. 6 Do not seek a treaty of friendship with them as long as you live. *The New International Version* (Grand Rapids, MI: Zondervan, 2011), Dt 23:3–6.

At that time Jesus went through the grainfields on the Sabbath. His disciples were hungry and began to pick some heads of grain and eat them. 2 When the Pharisees saw this, they said to him, "Look! Your disciples are doing what is unlawful on the Sabbath." 3 He answered, "Haven't you read what David did when he and his companions were hungry? 4 He entered the house of God, and he and his companions ate the consecrated bread—which was not lawful for them to do, but only for the priests. 5 Or haven't you read in the Law that the priests on Sabbath duty in the temple desecrate the Sabbath and yet are innocent? 6 I tell you that something greater than the temple is here. 7 If you had known what these words mean, 'I desire mercy, not sacrifice,' you would not have condemned the innocent. 8 For the Son of Man is Lord of the Sabbath." *The New International Version* (Grand Rapids, MI: Zondervan, 2011), Mt 12:1–8.

6 On another Sabbath he went into the synagogue and was teaching, and a man was there whose right hand was shriveled. 7 The Pharisees and the teachers of the law were looking for a reason to accuse Jesus, so they watched him closely to see if he would heal on the Sabbath. 8 But Jesus knew what they were thinking and said to the man with the shriveled hand, "Get up and stand in front of everyone." So he got up and stood there. 9 Then Jesus said to them, "I ask you, which is lawful on the Sabbath: to do good or to do evil, to save life or to destroy it?" 10 He looked around at them all, and then said to the man, "Stretch out your hand." He did so, and his hand was completely restored. 11 But the Pharisees and the teachers of the law were furious and began to discuss with one another what they might do to Jesus. *The New International Version* (Grand Rapids, MI: Zondervan, 2011), Lk 6:6–11.

27 Then he said to them, "The Sabbath was made for man, not man for the Sabbath. 28 So the Son of Man is Lord even of the Sabbath." *The New International Version* (Grand Rapids, MI: Zondervan, 2011), Mk 2:27–28.

8 If we claim to be without sin, we deceive ourselves and the truth is not in us. 9 If we confess our sins, he is faithful and just and will forgive us our sins and purify us from all unrighteousness. *The New International Version* (Grand Rapids, MI: Zondervan, 2011), 1 Jn 1:8–9.

Biblical Characters Who Are A Part Of Season 2 Episode 6
Unlawful

Ahimelek

Ahimelek is an actual priest found in 1 Samuel. He does provide David with bread for himself and for his alleged troops. In the Scriptures however, Ahimelek is much more afraid of the presence of David than is portrayed in the episode. This encounter that he has with David will cost him his life.

David

David is an actual person found in 1 Samuel. He does got to Ahimelek to request food and any weapons that might be on hand. David is actually fleeing from Saul, and nothing that he says to Ahimelek is the truth. The episode does portray David accurately as shown in the Scriptures.

Simon, Matthew, Mary Magdalene, Mary The Mother of Jesus, Andrew, Simon The Zealot, Thomas, James, John, and Philip

These are all actual biblical characters, but the event centered around Mary Magdalene's return is not recorded in the Scriptures, therefore none of the dialogue is an actual part of the Scriptures. The author is simply providing character development and depth of personalities for each. John the Baptist was actually arrested by Herod, but the Scriptures do not record the reactions of the disciples to the arrest. The disciples are given permission by Jesus to eat grain on the Sabbath.

Elam

Although the Scriptures do not record his name, there is an actual person whose arm was shriveled in a synagogue on the Sabbath. Jesus did tell the man to stretch out his arm and when he did, he was healed. There was anger expressed because the man had been healed on the Sabbath.

Jesus

Jesus is recorded in the Scriptures as giving the disciples permission to eat grain on the Sabbath, healing a man in the synagogue on the Sabbath, and quoting the passages in his conversations with the Pharisees and teachers of the law. The Scriptures do not record the conversation between Jesus and Mary Magdalene in this episode. The actions of Jesus on the Sabbath do cause greater tension between Jesus and the religious leaders. Jesus wants to drive home the point that He is Lord of the Sabbath.

Bible Study Discussion Questions Episode 6 Unlawful

1. The episode began with David lying to Abimelech. Eventually Abimelech will pay for this with his life. Has there been a time someone lied to you and it cost you a lot because you believed them?

2. Why do you think Simon insists on him and Matthew staying together while Matthew insists they should split up in their search for Mary?

3. Mary, Jesus' mother, spoke of being poor most of her life. Why does God allow those He has chosen to be poor?

4. Rhema said that she could not understand why Jesus would use Mary Magdalene's pain just to draw Simon and Matthew closer together. Has God ever used someone else's pain to help you see what it means to walk with Christ more clearly.

5. Is it possible for us to compel God to do anything? Why or Why not?

Helpful Guide To Understanding "The Chosen" Season 2

6. What does the verse "some trust in chariots, some in horses, but we will remember the name of the Lord our God" mean to you?

7. John mentioned he had wanted to join the Zealots, but felt he lacked the discipline. If you could go back and do one thing you had wanted to do, but didn't, what would it be?

8. The disciples were all puzzled by why Jesus sends Simon and Matthew to go an find Mary Magdalene when they didn't get along well with each other. Why do you think Jesus sent Simon and Matthew after her?

9. When Simon the Zealot hears that John has been arrested and was in prison, he wanted to contact some other zealots to go and break John out of prison. Why does Phillip remind him that was not an option? Has your anger ever tried to take you outside of the Kingdom of God ?

10. After Mary returned, Jesus asked if her if she really thought she would never sin or struggle again. What has changed about your view of you and your sin since you began walking with the Lord?

11. Jesus told Mary, "A redemption that could be lost in a day isn't much of a redemption." How secure do you feel in your walk with the Lord when you fail?

12. Thomas is almost obsessed with the possibility of them running out of food. How do you respond when it looks like you might not have enough of something you think you need?

13. Why do you think Matthew was listening to Mary and Jesus' conversation outside the tent?

14. If you had been Elam, and Jesus told you to stretch out your hand on the Sabbath, what if anything would cause you to hesitate?

15. Why did the Pharisees focus more on the Sabbath breaking than they did the healing? What cause us to sometimes be blind to the suffering of others?

16. Why did Jesus give the disciples permission to eat from the grainfields on the Sabbath?

17. What does it mean for you to know that Jesus is Lord of the Sabbath?

7 RESOURCES FOR EPISODE 7 RECKONING

Season 2 Episode 7 Reckoning
43 minutes Viewing Time

Main Characters

Atticus—the Roman who functions as a special military intelligence agent in the Roman government.

Quintus Dominus—Roman praetor in Capernaum who seeks Jesus for questioning and ultimately questions Jesus.

Simon, Andrew, John & Big James—the disciples sent out by Jesus to catch fish so that they can have food to eat.

Rabbi Shmuel—the Pharisee in search of testimony against Jesus.

Tamar—the Ethiopian woman who continues to preach about Jesus and what she has seen him do.

Gaius—the Roman commander who goes to arrest Jesus and was once Matthew's guard when he was a tax collector.

Phillip and Andrew—the disciples who go looking for Jesus after Jesus is arrested.

Rabbi Joseph—the Pharisee from Capernaum that comes with a

warning to be wary of Pharisee Shmuel and his motives.

The Disciples—they argue among themselves as to the best course of action to take now that Jesus has been arrested.

Jesus—the one who is calm about the possibility of being arrested while determined to work on a major sermon.

Summary of Episode 7 Reckoning

The episode begins with postings of Jesus of Nazareth being wanted for questioning by the Roman officials. Atticus goes to see Praetor Quintus Dominus over the postings. Atticus is concerned with what Jesus might do if he's arrested and how the people might react. Quintus is determined to have Jesus brought in so that he can question him for himself.

Jesus sends Andrew, Simon, Big James and John on a fishing trip so that they can catch some food for them to eat. The two brothers have a rock throwing contest to see who will actually go on the lake and fish, and who will return back to the camp to listen to what Jesus might have to say. Simon and Andrew lose the contest.

Jesus is working on a sermon. His goal is to have a message that not only will interest people, but will apply to each of their lives as well. Jesus wants to present them with truths that will define his ministry and help them to understand the kingdom of God.

Pharisee Shmuel and his partner return to Capernaum and speaks to Pharisee Joseph to find the Ethiopian woman who had brought her friend to be healed by Jesus. Shmuel wants testimony from her to use it against Jesus. The woman's name is Tamar. Shmuel also wants to find the leper that Jesus had healed. Pharisee Joseph is opposed to Shmuel's plans. Shmuel and his friends also go to the Romans to see Quintus to report where they have seen Jesus.

They do not get a warm reception from the Romans.

Gaius is sent to find Jesus and arrest him. Atticus goes with him and warns Gaius to expect the unexpected. Atticus knows of many of the miraculous things Jesus has done, and he's certain that Jesus could do something dramatic if arrested. Atticus does not think Jesus is a threat, but he is unsure of what he might do.

Simon and Andrew argue over whether Jesus is bringing too much attention to himself. Jesus appears to cause a scene everywhere they go. Andrew is afraid that Jesus' fate will be the same as John the Baptist's fate.

The disciples see the Roman soldiers coming toward Jesus. Jesus assures the disciples to be calm and to wait for him to come back. Gaius and Jesus have a talk, and Jesus assures Gaius that Matthew is doing well. Jesus agrees to go with him and the soldiers to be questioned.

The disciples argue over what steps to take next. Some want to go and set Jesus free, while others want to obey Jesus and wait for him to return as he told them to do. Andrew is adamant about going after Jesus, and Philip goes with him to calm Andrew down.

On their search, they run into Tamar and a person healed by Jesus, preaching in the square telling others what Jesus has done for them. They take them aside to tell them they must stop talking about Jesus because the Romans have already arrested him. They are eventually warned by Pharisee Joseph not to talk to Pharisee Shmuel. Pharisee Joseph comes to them in disguise, and Andrew is reluctant to trust him. Tamar and the man healed agree to go in hiding. Tamar goes with Andrew and Phillip to follow Jesus.

Quintus Dominus and Jesus have a cordial discussion among themselves. Dominus wants Jesus to stop stirring up things. Jesus will not promise that, and Dominus will not promise that he will not kill Jesus if it becomes necessary. Dominus does tell Jesus that he is sorry to hear about his cousin being arrested. He asks Jesus if he knows what he's getting himself into. Jesus is allowed to leave on his own, and he returns to the disciples, but not before going to spend some time in prayer alone.

Pharisee Shmuel and his companions run into two rabbis who have evidence against Jesus. They were leaders in the synagogue in which Jesus had healed the man with the withered hand on the Sabbath, and they had seen the disciples eating grain in the fields on the Sabbath. Shmuel is very interested in their testimony.

Jesus returns to the camp later that evening. The disciples all want to know what happened with the Romans. Jesus reminds them that he told them that he would be back. Big James is upset that Jesus went off to pray before returning to them after his time with the Roman interrogation. Jesus lets them know that if they have a hard time trusting him now, it's going to be far more difficult after he is gone. The episode concludes with Jesus teaching them the Lord's prayer. The final scene has Jesus seeking Matthew's help in writing his big sermon.

Scriptures Woven Into Episode 7 Reckoning

14 Indignant because Jesus had healed on the Sabbath, the synagogue leader said to the people, "There are six days for work. So come and be healed on those days, not on the Sabbath." *The New International Version* (Grand Rapids, MI: Zondervan, 2011), Lk 13:14.

After Jesus was born in Bethlehem in Judea, during the time of King Herod, Magi from the east came to Jerusalem 2 and asked, "Where is the one who has been born king of the Jews? We saw his star when it rose and have come to worship him." *The New International Version* (Grand Rapids, MI: Zondervan, 2011), Mt 2:1–2.

9 After they had heard the king, they went on their way, and the star they had seen when it rose went ahead of them until it stopped over the place where the child was. 10 When they saw the star, they were overjoyed. 11 On coming to the house, they saw the child with his mother Mary, and they bowed down and worshiped him. Then they opened their treasures and presented him with gifts of gold,

frankincense and myrrh. *The New International Version* (Grand Rapids, MI: Zondervan, 2011), Mt 2:9–11.

24 News about him spread all over Syria, and people brought to him all who were ill with various diseases, those suffering severe pain, the demon-possessed, those having seizures, and the paralyzed; and he healed them. 25 Large crowds from Galilee, the Decapolis, Jerusalem, Judea and the region across the Jordan followed him. *The New International Version* (Grand Rapids, MI: Zondervan, 2011), Mt 4:24–25.

3 Now Herod had arrested John and bound him and put him in prison because of Herodias, his brother Philip's wife, 4 for John had been saying to him: "It is not lawful for you to have her." 5 Herod wanted to kill John, but he was afraid of the people, because they considered John a prophet. *The New International Version* (Grand Rapids, MI: Zondervan, 2011), Mt 14:3–5.

23 One Sabbath Jesus was going through the grainfields, and as his disciples walked along, they began to pick some heads of grain. 24 The Pharisees said to him, "Look, why are they doing what is unlawful on the Sabbath?" 25 He answered, "Have you never read what David did when he and his companions were hungry and in need? 26 In the days of Abiathar the high priest, he entered the house of God and ate the consecrated bread, which is lawful only for priests to eat. And he also gave some to his companions." 27 Then he said to them, "The Sabbath was made for man, not man for the Sabbath. 28 So the Son of Man is Lord even of the Sabbath." *The New International Version* (Grand Rapids, MI: Zondervan, 2011), Mk 2:23–28.

9 "This, then, is how you should pray: " 'Our Father in heaven, hallowed be your name, 10 your kingdom come, your will be done, on earth as it is in heaven. 11 Give us today our daily bread. 12 And forgive us our debts, as we also have forgiven our debtors. 13 And lead us not into temptation, but deliver us from the evil one. *The New International Version* (Grand Rapids, MI: Zondervan, 2011), Mt 6:9–13.

One day Jesus was praying in a certain place. When he finished, one of his disciples said to him, "Lord, teach us to pray, just as John taught his disciples." 2 He said to them, "When you pray, say: " 'Father, hallowed be your name, your kingdom come. 3 Give us each day our daily bread. 4 Forgive us our sins, for we also forgive everyone who sins against us. And lead us not into temptation.' " *The New International Version* (Grand Rapids, MI: Zondervan, 2011), Lk 11:1–4.

Biblical Characters Who Are A Part Of Season 2 Episode 7 Reckoning

Andrew, Simon, James, John, Mary, Mary Magdalene, Matthew, Simon the Zealot, Thaddeus, James, Thomas

Episode 7 is built around the story of Jesus being arrested and interrogated by the Roman officials. The Scriptures do not record Jesus being arrested by the Roman government during his ministry. So none of the dialogue or the events depicted by the disciples in this episode can be found in the Bible with one exception. The disciples do ask Jesus to teach them to pray as John taught his disciples to pray.

Jesus

The Scriptures do not record the Romans arresting Jesus during his ministry. Jesus is told on one occasion by the Pharisees to leave the area because Herod wants to kill him in Luke's gospel chapter 13. Jesus does make a reference to the wise men from the east coming to visit him as a child. Jesus's desire to go off by himself to pray is consistent with the Scriptures. Jesus's warning to the disciples that he will not always be with them is a part of the Scriptures. Jesus does teach the disciples, what has become known as the Lord's prayer, and it is recorded by Matthew and Luke.

Bible Study Discussion Questions Episode 7 Reckoning

1. When was a time you had to face an authority figure to give an account for your actions, and how did you feel leading up to the appointment?

2. What do you think makes for a good sermon?

3. The Pharisee Shmuel is determined to find Jesus guilty of something at almost any cost. What do you think is at the root of his desire?

4. Why do you think that Andrew is so afraid of "what might happen" to Jesus? When we walk in fear of "what might happen" what does that say about our trust in God.

5. Atticus has witnessed Jesus do several kinds of miracles, and he warns Gaius to be careful in his attempt to arrest Jesus. How can people see miracles and still refuse to believe on Jesus?

6. Why do you think Jesus is so calm when the Romans come to arrest him in this episode?

Helpful Guide To Understanding "The Chosen" Season 2

7. Why do you think Jesus tells Gaius that Matthew is safe and doing well?

8. If you had been in the midst of the disciples after Jesus was arrested, which group would you naturally lean to; the group that wanted to do something or the group that wanted to wait?

9. Why do the disciples start to attack one another, especially the attack on Mary Magdalene?

10. Why do we attack one another as believers?

11. Tamar, the Ethiopian was introduced in a previous episode. What is her motivation for telling others about Jesus? What motivates you the most to tell others about Jesus?

12. When Jesus tells Quintus Dominus that he entertained guests once from the far east, what was he referring to in his life?

13. Dominus tells Jesus that Jesus is not what he expected. How has Jesus been different from what you expected when you first came to know Him?

14. Why do you think Jesus took the time to pray after his release instead of going directly to the disciples?

15. Which part of the Lord's prayer presents you with the most challenge in your life?

8 RESOURCES FOR EPISODE 8 BEYOND MOUNTAINS

Season 2 Episode 8 Beyond Mountains
59 Minutes Viewing Time

Main Characters

Negotiators—two men who seek to obtain what they want by working as a team of swindlers.

The Disciples—the disciples are all involved in getting preparations made for the sermon that Jesus is going to give to the people. They are all somewhat nervous about their responsibilities.

Shmuel—the Pharisee still seeking to build a case against Jesus for false prophecy.

Matthew—the disciple who was a former tax collector whom Jesus has chosen to help him with the organization of Jesus's sermon.

Barnaby—the man who leads a woman who is blind and is a close friend of the disciples from the early days of the ministry.

Mary—Jesus' mother whom he calls "Imma."

Jesus—the one who is preparing to deliver a sermon that will be remembered for ages.

Summary of Season 2 Episode 7 Beyond Mountains

The episode begins with three men out on a hillside negotiating for the price of a piece of land. The owner is reluctant to sell his family land which has been theirs for 40 generations. The other two men are working together to scheme the man out of the true value of the land. They tell him they want the land for burial plots they want to sell, but they in fact know there is salt under the land worth a fortune.

The disciples are in camp beginning preparations for a sermon Jesus is to preach. John and James are cutting wood. Simon the Zealot is exercising, Phillip and Thomas bring apples for breakfast. Matthew is on assignment with Jesus. Thaddeus, Little James, and Nathanael are off searching for a sight for Jesus to preach his upcoming sermon. Jesus wants a location that has a view of the Sea of Galilee.

Mary Magdalene is teaching Rhema to read from Psalm 139. Mary is also writing out flyers for the upcoming sermon. Thomas wants Tamar to let Rhema know he has found some apricots just for her. Thomas also explains to Tamar that the arguing among the disciples is really a form of love.

The younger of the two negotiators has second misgivings over having cheated the man out of his property. The older one tries to convince him that they have done nothing wrong. The younger one is being trained as an apprentice, but he wants more out of life than just money. He desires to do something in life that he can be proud of and remembered throughout history. He acknowledges that the One True King is in heaven.

Shmuel continues going to different authorities in his pursuit of declaring Jesus a false prophet. But the person he goes to is only interested in humiliating his opponents, including Nicodemus, for political gain. Jesus is simply a means to an end to destroy his political rivals.

Jesus uses Matthew to get feedback for the sermon he is going to preach. When Jesus asks Matthew for his opinion, Matthew points out that the sermon seems to have more negative news than good news. Jesus explains his goal is to start a revolution, not be sentimental. Jesus explains why he uses the phrase you are the salt of the earth. Jesus emphasizes he does not want passive followers. Matthew is concerned that Jesus is concerned about the other disciples in the camp. Matthew just wishes everyone would get along better. Jesus says he knew there would be conflict when he opened up the kingdom to everyone.

The disciples are posting and passing out flyers to all who will take them. Negotiations do not go well for James, Thaddeus, and Nethanael with the owner of the site for the sermon location. Fortunately, the two negotiators are there, and they point out to the owner of the land how he could benefit from having the event on his property. The owner agrees to the use of the land as long as the disciples clean up everything afterwards. The two negotiators disappear before the disciples, can thank them.

The flyers reach people from all walks of life including the negotiators, Gaius, Atticus, Quintus Dominus, Zebedee, Simon's wife Eden, and Barnaby a friend of the disciples. The negotiators decide they want to hear Jesus speak along with many others.

Jesus and Matthew finalize the work on the sermon. Jesus decides to start with a road map on where people could find him. He will open with "Blessed are the….". As he recites each of the Beatitudes, the camera shows which of the disciples fall into the category of the trait that is being cited.

The big moment is arriving. The women want to dress Jesus in something a little more colorful to be better seen by the people. Rhema, Mary his mother, Mary Magdalene and Tamar each have a reason for the color they have chosen. When Jesus asks them to choose the color, it is a tie vote 2-2. Simon's wife, Eden, shows up, and Jesus asks her to be the tie breaker.

Jesus and his mother Mary share a moment of joy and sorrow together. Both have feelings about Joseph not being there. Jesus demonstrates his sense of humor when Mary tells him how proud she is of him.

Barnaby and his friend are followed by the younger negotiator to where the disciples are. Nathanael recognizes the younger negotiator and takes him to Peter explaining that he had helped them to get the spot for the sermon. Nathanael introduces the young man as Judas to Simon. Simon welcomes Judas to the event.

The episode concludes with Jesus walking in slow motion past his disciples as he heads to the platform to preach, The Sermon On The Mount.

Scriptures Woven Into Season 2 Episode 8 Beyond Mountains

7 No inheritance in Israel is to pass from one tribe to another, for every Israelite shall keep the tribal inheritance of their ancestors. *The New International Version* (Grand Rapids, MI: Zondervan, 2011), Nu 36:6–7.

13 For you created my inmost being; you knit me together in my mother's womb. 14 I praise you because I am fearfully and wonderfully made; your works are wonderful, I know that full well. 15 My frame was not hidden from you when I was made in the secret place, when I was woven together in the depths of the earth. 16 Your eyes saw my unformed body; all the days ordained for me were written in your book before one of them came to be. *The New International Version* (Grand Rapids, MI: Zondervan, 2011), Ps 139:13–16.

3 "Blessed are the poor in spirit, for theirs is the kingdom of heaven.

4 Blessed are those who mourn, for they will be comforted. 5 Blessed are the meek, for they will inherit the earth. 6 Blessed are those who hunger and thirst for righteousness, for they will be filled. 7 Blessed are the merciful, for they will be shown mercy. 8 Blessed are the pure in heart, for they will see God. 9 Blessed are the peacemakers, for they will be called children of God. 10 Blessed are those who are persecuted because of righteousness, for theirs is the kingdom of heaven. 11 "Blessed are you when people insult you, persecute you and falsely say all kinds of evil against you because of me. 12 Rejoice and be glad, because great is your reward in heaven, for in the same way they persecuted the prophets who were before you. *The New International Version* (Grand Rapids, MI: Zondervan, 2011), Mt 5:3–12.

13 "You are the salt of the earth. But if the salt loses its saltiness, how can it be made salty again? It is no longer good for anything, except to be thrown out and trampled underfoot. *The New International Version* (Grand Rapids, MI: Zondervan, 2011), Mt 5:13.

27 "You have heard that it was said, 'You shall not commit adultery.' 28 But I tell you that anyone who looks at a woman lustfully has already committed adultery with her in his heart. 29 If your right eye causes you to stumble, gouge it out and throw it away. It is better for you to lose one part of your body than for your whole body to be thrown into hell. 30 And if your right hand causes you to stumble, cut it off and throw it away. It is better for you to lose one part of your body than for your whole body to go into hell. *The New International Version* (Grand Rapids, MI: Zondervan, 2011), Mt 5:27–31.

43 "You have heard that it was said, 'Love your neighbor and hate your enemy.' 44 But I tell you, love your enemies and pray for those who persecute you, 45 that you may be children of your Father in heaven. He causes his sun to rise on the evil and the good, and sends rain on the righteous and the unrighteous. *The New International Version* (Grand Rapids, MI: Zondervan, 2011), Mt 5:43–45.

13 This is why I speak to them in parables: "Though seeing, they do

not see; though hearing, they do not hear or understand. 14 In them is fulfilled the prophecy of Isaiah: " 'You will be ever hearing but never understanding; you will be ever seeing but never perceiving. 15 For this people's heart has become calloused; they hardly hear with their ears, and they have closed their eyes. Otherwise they might see with their eyes, hear with their ears, understand with their hearts and turn, and I would heal them .*The New International Version* (Grand Rapids, MI: Zondervan, 2011), Mt 13:13–15.

Biblical Characters Who Are A Part Of Season 2 Episode 8 Beyond Mountains

The Disciples Simon, Andrew, Big James, John, Thomas, James, Phillip, Simon the Zealot, Matthew, Thaddeus, Nathanael

They are all in this episode, however the Scriptures do not record any events of their activities leading up to Jesus preaching the message known as the Sermon on the Mount.

Mary Magdalene, Zebedee, Simon's wife Eden

They are all in this episode, however the Scriptures do not record any events of their activities leading up to Jesus preaching the message known as the Sermon on the Mount.

Judas

Judas appears for the first time in this episode and is recorded in the Scriptures as Judas Iscariot. The Scriptures do not record the circumstances under which Judas came to meet the other disciples.

Jesus

Jesus does quote many of the verses preparing for his sermon that do become a part of the Sermon on the Mount. The Scriptures do not record Matthew assisting with the preparation of the sermon. Several of the statements that Jesus makes are consistent with principles found in the Scriptures.

Bible Study Discussion Questions Season 2

Episode 8 Beyond Mountains

1. This episode involved everyone preparing for Jesus' big opening sermon. What big event did you help to prepare for that meant a lot to you?

2. The opening of the episode involved a man being swindled out of his property. How should followers of Christ respond when they know someone is being cheated? If a believer is selling a car, what duty does he or she have to reveal all the things wrong with the car?

3. John and James are cutting wood for the sole purpose of leaving it behind for the next travelers who might come that way? Can you think of anything you do to intentionally be a blessing to someone who is coming behind you whom you may never meet?

4. Mary Magdalene is using her knowledge of how to read to teach Rhema to read the Scriptures? Can you think of how you are investing in someone else's life to help them grow in Christ?

5. The disciples were arguing among themselves, but Thomas tells Tamar they are actually loving each other. When is disagreement loving among believers?

Helpful Guide To Understanding "The Chosen" Season 2

6. The disciples are completely failing in their bid to get the owner to allow them to use his property for Jesus' sermon. In comes the involvement of two strangers who helps them complete the deal. When has God used a perfect stranger or strangers to open a door for you that seemed shut?

7. The younger of the two negotiators wants to be remembered in history in such a way that he could be proud of it. How do you want history to remember you?

8. Jesus tells Matthew that he knew conflict would be inevitable if everyone was invited into his kingdom. How does inviting everyone into the church causes conflict today?

9. Jesus tells Mathew that he came to start a revolution, but not a revolt. What do you see as the difference between the two as it relates to our society today?

10. Why are we called to be the salt of the earth? If someone was to ask you, when was the last time you were acting like salt, what would be your response?

11. What do you think is the difference between a passive follower of Christ and an active follower of Christ? Is there such a thing as a passive follower of Jesus?

12. Thomas is nervous about not doing all that he can to make things the best for Jesus. Have you ever felt you were not quite doing enough for Jesus? If so, where are those feelings coming from?

13. Jesus goes through the Beatitudes while the camera panned the different people to whom they applied. Which of the Beatitudes do you think you fit in the most?

14. It seems it is a mere coincidence that Judas happens to run into Barnaby who leads him to Thaddeus? Have you ever had a coincidence lead to a life changing experience for you? How do you think God feels about coincidences?

15. Jesus and his mother both share how they miss Joseph. Mary regrets he is not there to see this moment. What moment in your life did you wish someone you loved could have been there to see it, but they were no longer alive?

16. How did you feel watching Jesus going to the stage to preach at the end of the episode?

9 RESOURCES FOR CHRISTMAS SPECIAL MESSENGERS

Season 2 Christmas Special Episode Messengers

39 minutes

Main Characters

Joseph & Mary—the parents of Jesus on their way to Bethlehem.

Mary—the mother of Jesus who gives an account after the resurrection has taken place.

Lazarus—the man Jesus raised from the dead and is housing Mary, the mother of Jesus.

Mary Magdalene—the disciple of Jesus who comes to see Mary, the mother of Jesus who is ill.

Luke—the disciple of Jesus who is gathering the facts to write a historical account of the life and resurrection of Jesus.

Summary of Christmas Special Episode Messengers

In this episode, there is a constant changing of going from the year 48 AD which would be after the death of Jesus, and 4 BC which would be around the time Jesus would have been born. The episode begins with a man pulling a cart headed toward the city in the year 48. He sees Roman soldiers guarding the entrance to the city. He puts on a cloak and says a prayer as he heads to the city. Persecution has broken out against the church at this point in history.

The next scene occurs in 4AD with Mary and Joseph traveling

on the road to Bethlehem to be counted in the census. Mary is riding a donkey and wants to get off. She thanks Joseph for standing by her side in the midst of their difficult situation. Joseph tells her God told him to do it and that he was happy about it. They refer to each other's messenger (angel) who came to them. Mary's messenger had told her nothing was impossible with God. Joseph's messenger had told him that Mary would give birth to a son and they were to call him Jesus.'

The scene goes back to 48 AD and the traveler is stopped at the gate by the Roman soldier who inspects his cargo. His papers are in order so he is allowed to enter the city. The wagon he is using has a false bottom to it, and the traveler has a secret passenger.

The scene goes back to Mary and Joseph. Joseph is having difficulty securing a place for them to stay. Joseph cannot remember exactly where his friend Samuel lived in Bethlehem.

The scene shifts to 48 AD with the stranger. He goes to Lazarus' home and provides a secret symbol of a half of a fish to establish his identity in the sand in front of the door. Lazarus completes the other half of the fish to establish his identity. Lazarus is protecting Mary, the mother of Jesus in his home.

The scene shifts back to Mary and Joseph. Joseph is doing his best to negotiate a price for a room. Mary begins to quote one of the psalms because of her thirst. She needs water. The scene flashes to Mary many years later as they share the same prayer together. Joseph is offered the opportunity to stay in a stable and he takes it.

The stranger with the cart has smuggled in Mary Magdalene in the cart with the false bottom. She has come first to see how Mary is doing because Mary has been ill and second because Mary had requested her presence. The reunion between the two women is a joyous moment. The church is under persecution and Mary wants to know what is happening to the other disciples which she refers to as her boys. Mary provides both good and bad news. Big James and Nathanael have been killed. Andrew is about to be arrested, the rest are scattered and preaching the gospel. Mary wants Mary Magdalene to get in touch with Luke.

The scene goes back to Joseph and Mary in the stable. Mary goes into labor. She recites her song, "My Soul Magnifies the Lord." Joseph notices a strange color in the sky looking through a window. Joseph delivers the Mary. The scene goes back and forth in time as the older Mary remembers the song, "My soul magnifies the Lord."

The older Mary wants Mary Magdalene to deliver her song to Luke along with a story about the swaddling clothes. She wants Luke to be able to include them in the stories he's writing about Jesus. She also presents Mary Magdalene with a special gift. Mary has kept the swaddling clothes all these years. Before Mary Magdalene leaves, she gives her the blessing, "The Lord bless you and keep you." They know they might not see each other again. Mary Magdalene goes and finds Luke to present him with the additional material from Mary.

Scriptures Woven Into Episode Christmas Special Messengers

18 This is how the birth of Jesus the Messiah came about: His mother Mary was pledged to be married to Joseph, but before they came together, she was found to be pregnant through the Holy Spirit. 19 Because Joseph her husband was faithful to the law, and yet did not want to expose her to public disgrace, he had in mind to divorce her quietly. 20 But after he had considered this, an angel of the Lord appeared to him in a dream and said, "Joseph son of David, do not be afraid to take Mary home as your wife, because what is conceived in her is from the Holy Spirit. 21 She will give birth to a son, and you are to give him the name Jesus, because he will save his people from their sins." 22 All this took place to fulfill what the Lord had said through the prophet: 23 "The virgin will conceive and give birth to a son, and they will call him Immanuel" (which means "God with us"). 24 When Joseph woke up, he did what the angel of the Lord had commanded him and took Mary home as his wife. 25 But he did not consummate their marriage until she gave birth to a son. And he gave him the name Jesus. *The New International Version* (Grand Rapids, MI: Zondervan, 2011), Mt 1:18–25.

26 In the sixth month of Elizabeth's pregnancy, God sent the angel Gabriel to Nazareth, a town in Galilee, 27 to a virgin pledged to be married to a man named Joseph, a descendant of David. The virgin's name was Mary. 28 The angel went to her and said, "Greetings, you who are highly favored! The Lord is with you." 29 Mary was greatly troubled at his words and wondered what kind of greeting this might be. 30 But the angel said to her, "Do not be afraid, Mary; you have

found favor with God. 31 You will conceive and give birth to a son, and you are to call him Jesus. 32 He will be great and will be called the Son of the Most High. The Lord God will give him the throne of his father David, 33 and he will reign over Jacob's descendants forever; his kingdom will never end." 34 "How will this be," Mary asked the angel, "since I am a virgin?" 35 The angel answered, "The Holy Spirit will come on you, and the power of the Most High will overshadow you. So the holy one to be born will be called the Son of God. 36 Even Elizabeth your relative is going to have a child in her old age, and she who was said to be unable to conceive is in her sixth month. 37 For no word from God will ever fail." 38 "I am the Lord's servant," Mary answered. "May your word to me be fulfilled." Then the angel left her. *The New International Version* (Grand Rapids, MI: Zondervan, 2011), Lk 1:26–38.

39 At that time Mary got ready and hurried to a town in the hill country of Judea, 40 where she entered Zechariah's home and greeted Elizabeth. 41 When Elizabeth heard Mary's greeting, the baby leaped in her womb, and Elizabeth was filled with the Holy Spirit. 42 In a loud voice she exclaimed: "Blessed are you among women, and blessed is the child you will bear! 43 But why am I so favored, that the mother of my Lord should come to me? 44 As soon as the sound of your greeting reached my ears, the baby in my womb leaped for joy. 45 Blessed is she who has believed that the Lord would fulfill his promises to her!" *The New International Version* (Grand Rapids, MI: Zondervan, 2011), Lk 1:39–45.

46 And Mary said: "My soul glorifies the Lord 47 and my spirit rejoices in God my Savior, 48 for he has been mindful of the humble state of his servant. From now on all generations will call me blessed, 49 for the Mighty One has done great things for me— holy is his name. 50 His mercy extends to those who fear him, from generation to generation. 51 He has performed mighty deeds with his arm; he has scattered those who are proud in their inmost thoughts. 52 He has brought down rulers from their thrones but has lifted up the humble. 53 He has filled the hungry with good things but has sent the rich away empty. 54 He has helped his servant Israel, remembering to be merciful 55 to Abraham and his descendants forever, just as he promised our ancestors." *The New*

International Version (Grand Rapids, MI: Zondervan, 2011), Lk 1:46–55.

14 Therefore the Lord himself will give you a sign: The virgin will conceive and give birth to a son, and will call him Immanuel. *The New International Version* (Grand Rapids, MI: Zondervan, 2011), Is 7:14.

As the deer pants for streams of water, so my soul pants for you, my God. 2 My soul thirsts for God, for the living God. When can I go and meet with God? *The New International Version* (Grand Rapids, MI: Zondervan, 2011), Ps 42:1–2.

4 So Joseph also went up from the town of Nazareth in Galilee to Judea, to Bethlehem the town of David, because he belonged to the house and line of David. 5 He went there to register with Mary, who was pledged to be married to him and was expecting a child. 6 While they were there, the time came for the baby to be born, 7 and she gave birth to her firstborn, a son. She wrapped him in cloths and placed him in a manger, because there was no guest room available for them.
The New International Version (Grand Rapids, MI: Zondervan, 2011), Lk 2:4–7.

" ' "The Lord bless you and keep you; 25 the Lord make his face shine on you and be gracious to you; 26 the Lord turn his face toward you and give you peace." ' *The New International Version* (Grand Rapids, MI: Zondervan, 2011), Nu 6:24–26.

1 Many have undertaken to draw up an account of the things that have been fulfilled among us, 2 just as they were handed down to us by those who from the first were eyewitnesses and servants of the word. 3 With this in mind, since I myself have carefully investigated everything from the beginning, I too decided to write an orderly account for you, most excellent Theophilus, 4 so that you may know the certainty of the things you have been taught. *The New International Version* (Grand Rapids, MI: Zondervan, 2011), Lk 1:1–4.

Biblical Characters Who Are Part of Episode Christmas Special-Messengers

Joseph & Mary

Joseph and Mary are actually recorded in the Scriptures as traveling to Bethlehem during the time of the census. They were not able to secure lodging at an inn, so they did spend the night in a stable in which Mary gave birth to Jesus. The messengers that came to each of them are also recorded in the Scriptures as well as the prophecies they mention. Mary did write a song after her visit to Elizabeth.

Mary

Mary the mother of Jesus is recorded in the Scriptures after she gave birth to Jesus. The last time the Scriptures mention her is in Acts as part of the group waiting in Jerusalem for the Holy Spirit on the day of Pentecost. The Scriptures do not record the events in the episode with Mary and Mary Magdalene. It is very likely that Luke did receive some of the material from his gospel directly from Mary since he was looking for eye-witness accounts.

Mary Magdalene

Mary Magdalene is recorded in the Scriptures on several occasions. The last mention of her by name is after the resurrection of Jesus. The Scriptures do not record any of the events of Mary Magdalene in this episode. However, the church would have been under persecution at this point in history, and the Scriptures do record that Big James has been killed by Herod for his faith. The Scriptures also record that the disciples had scattered all over after the breakout of persecution.

Luke

Luke is recoded in the Scriptures as the one who gathered first hand accounts in preparation for writing about Jesus and the early church. The Scriptures do not record Mary Magdalene actually taking a manuscript from Mary to Luke.

Lazarus

Lazarus is recorded in the Scriptures as having been raised from the dead by Jesus. The last mention of Lazarus in the Scripture was that the religious leaders wanted to put him to death because people were believing in Jesus because of Lazarus' resurrection. The Scriptures do not record Lazarus hiding Mary in his home.

Bible Study Discussion Questions Episode Christmas Special Messengers

1. Do you think Mary understood the cost that would be involved when she said yes to the angel Gabriel about giving birth to Jesus?

2. What unexpected loss did you incur at a time when you said yes to God?

3. Who do you think was carrying the greater burden with the news of Mary being pregnant, Mary or Joseph? Why?

4. Why do you think God did not answer their prayer for a room to be available at the inn?

5. Has there been a time in your life when God disregarded a prayer in your life for comfort for a greater purpose?

6. What do you think is the purpose of persecution in the life of the church?

7. Mary Magdalene mentioned the death of Big James. What do you think came out of James' death?

8. If you had of been Joseph, would you have been comfortable delivering the baby alone with your wife? Why or why not?

9. How do we know that we can trust the stories about the birth of Christ?

10. What intrigues you the most about the biblical account of Christmas?

11. Christmas was not easy for Mary and Joseph? What makes Christmas difficult for you?

12. How does the birth of Jesus show the love God has for us?

10 MEET THE AUTHOR

MEET THE AUTHOR

Rick Gillespie-Mobley has been a committed evangelical pastor since 1983. He currently is a part of A Covenant Order Of Evangelical Presbyterians (ECO). He is a gifted communicator and uses stories and humor in his messages in a way that engages his audiences. He has an extensive Christian background in several Christian denominations that include charismatics, Methodists, Church of God In Christ, Full Gospel, United Church Of Christ, Assemblies of God and Presbyterians.

Rick has a true love for the Scriptures as being the word of God and the authoritative interpretation for how we should live our lives today.

His background as a lawyer has given him a unique way of analyzing the text in addition to the way he learned at seminary. He has put together this guide to help people to find the richness in the Chosen Series. If one is not aware of the Scriptures, some of the things in the series will just zip past you. Rick has gathered the Scriptures referred to in each episode along with a summary of each episode to assist people in watching the series. The group discussion questions are designed to allow for almost anyone to lead a discussion on the series.

Rick was married on August 30, 1980 to his bride Toby. They served together as co-pastors for nearly 38 years. In addition to their adult children Samantha, Anita (Milan), Keon (Ashley), and Sharon, they have served as foster parents for 20 years. Rick is a graduate of Hornell Senior High School in Hornell, NY, Hamilton College B.A. in Clinton, NY, Gordon Conwel Theological Seminary M. Div. in S. Hamilton, MA, Trinity Bible College & Seminary D. Min in Newburgh, IN and Boston University School of Law J.D in Boston, MA.

Rick has served with his wife Toby as co-pastors of Roxbury Presbyterian Church (6 years) in Boston, Ma, and Glenville New Life Community Church (24 years).

They also served as pastors in Cleveland, Oh at New Life Fellowship (4 Years) in Cleveland, OH, Calvary Presbyterian Church (2 years), and New Life At Calvary (8 years). Toby was honorably retired in 2020 and Rick was honorably retired in 2021.. Rick and Toby were both ordained in the Presbyterian Church of the United States Of America, but transferred their membership to A Covenant Order of Evangelical Presbyterian (ECO). Rick was admitted to practice law in both Massachusetts and Ohio.

Other books by Rick Gillespie-Mobley Include The Following:

20 Small Group Bible Studies

Easter Comes Alive

Why Can't A Woman Preach, Teach, Pastor Or Be An Apostle

Christmas: What Child Is This (Drama)

Five Mother's Day or Women's Day Sermons

Rich Black History Sermons: Africans In The Bible

The Play: Easter Comes Alive With The Resurrection

The Eye Of The Pastor: 11 Stories You Should Have Been Told Before You Started Ministry

Five Sermons For Father's Day Of Men's Day

Is God In The Crisis: From Triage To Transformation

Helpful Guide To Understanding "The Chosen" Season 1

Helpful Guide To Understanding "The Chosen" Season 2

Growing In Christ Through The Book Of James: 12 Bible Studies

The Art Of Becoming Ushers and Greeters

The Art Of Writing A Eulogy

Made in the USA
Monee, IL
02 January 2025